CHANGED HEART, CHANGED WORLD

Other Books by William Barry

Contemplatives in Action: The Jesuit Way
(with Robert G. Doherty)

Finding God in All Things:
A Companion to the Spiritual Exercises of St. Ignatius

A Friendship Like No Other:
Experiencing God's Amazing Embrace

God and You: Prayer as a Personal Relationship

God's Passionate Desire

A Hunger for God: Ten Approaches to Prayer
(edited with Kerry Maloney)

Letting God Come Close:
An Approach to the Ignatian Spiritual Exercises

Now Choose Life: Conversion as the Way to Life

Our Way of Proceeding:
To Make the Constitutions of the Society of Jesus and Their
Complementary Norms Our Own

Paying Attention to God: Discernment in Prayer

The Practice of Spiritual Direction
(with William J. Connolly)

Seek My Face: Prayer as Personal Relationship in Scripture

Spiritual Direction and the Encounter with God:
A Theological Inquiry

Take My Heart, Take My Hand: Living Fully in Friendship with God

What Do I Want in Prayer?

Who Do You Say I Am? Meeting the Historical Jesus in Prayer

With an Everlasting Love:
Developing an Intimate Relationship with God

CHANGED HEART, CHANGED WORLD

The Transforming Freedom of Friendship with God

William A. Barry, SJ

LOYOLA PRESS.
A JESUIT MINISTRY

Chicago

LOYOLA PRESS.
A JESUIT MINISTRY

3441 N. Ashland Avenue
Chicago, Illinois 60657
(800) 621-1008
www.loyolapress.com

Imprimi potest: Very Reverend Myles N. Sheehan, SJ, provincial

Unless otherwise noted, the Scripture quotations contained herein are from the New Revised Standard Version Bible: Catholic Edition, copyright © 1993 and 1989 by the Division of Christian Education of the National Council of the Churches of Christ in the U.S.A. Used by permission. All rights reserved.

The quotations from *The Spiritual Exercises* are taken from St. Ignatius of Loyola, *Personal Writings*. Tr. and Ed. Joseph A. Munitiz and Philip Endean. London: Penguin Books, 1996.

"One Heart" by Franz Wright (pp. 70–71) is from *Walking to Martha's Vineyard*. New York: Alfred A. Knopf, 2004. Used with permission of the author.

"Would You Do the Same Today?" by Susan Kay (pp. 114–115) was published in Human Development 29, no. 2 (Summer 2008). Used with permission of the author.

"Compassion and Peace" by Edward Niziolek, SJ (pp. 117–118) is from *O Miraculous Wonder Help Us to Find You: Book II* (Arlington Heights, MA: Stephen Surette Graphic Services, 2008). Used with permission of the author.

"Rummaging for God: Praying Backward through Your Day" by Dennis Hamm (pp. 177–181) was published in America, May 14, 1994. Used with permission of the author.

Parts of chapters 1, 5, 6, 7 and 8 originally appeared in *Human Development*. Permission to reprint is gratefully acknowledged.

Cover image Getty Images: IIC/ Axiom

Library of Congress Cataloging-in-Publication Data
Barry, William A.
  Changed heart, changed world : the transforming freedom of friendship with God / William A. Barry.
      p. cm.
  Includes bibliographical references.
  ISBN-13: 978-0-8294-3303-6
  ISBN-10: 0-8294-3303-1
  1. Spirituality--Catholic Church. 2. Spiritual life--Catholic Church. 3. Christian life--Catholic authors. I. Title.
  BX2350.65.B37 2011
  248.4'82--dc22

                                                                      2010040256

Printed in the United States of America
        13 14 15 16 Versa 10 9 8 7 6 5 4 3 2

For Clare and Wallace Ritchie

Friends and Doers of the Word

Contents

Teach me to seek You,
and reveal Yourself to me as I seek;
for unless You instruct me
I cannot seek You,
and unless You reveal Yourself
I cannot find You.
Let me seek You in desiring You;
let me desire You in seeking You.
Let me find You in loving You;
let me love You in finding You.

—St. Anselm of Canterbury

Preface

Early in 2007, Father Agbonkianmeghe Orobator, SJ, then rector of the Jesuit community at Hekima College, in Nairobi, Kenya, invited me to give a lecture at the Hekima Forum for Exploring Faith in Public Life on December 15. I agreed to speak on the topic of friendship with God in the real world. The talk was well received. I was later invited to give the Loyola Lecture at St. Thomas Aquinas Parish at the University of Connecticut on March 22, 2008, where I was privileged to talk on the same topic. These invitations gave me the impetus to begin this book, an exploration of the ways friendship with God affects the worlds we live in. In the meantime, Guest House at Lake Orion, Michigan, invited me to give the keynote address at the fifty-ninth annual convention of the National Catholic Council on Alcoholism in Houston on January 20, 2009, a further impetus. I am grateful to the communities connected with Hekima College, St. Thomas Aquinas Parish in Storrs, Connecticut, and Guest House for these invitations, for the positive reception, and for insightful questions and observations that furthered my thinking and prayer on this topic.

A number of friends read the successive drafts of the book. I am very grateful to Robert G. Doherty, SJ; Kathleen Foley, SND; Kenneth J. Hughes, SJ; Robert E. Lindsay, SJ; Thomas J. Massaro, SJ; and William C. Russell, SJ—all of whom read with kindness and acumen and helped me make the end product much better than its beginnings. Vinita Hampton Wright of Loyola Press has been very helpful in making the book more user friendly. I am grateful to readers of articles in *Human Development* who encouraged me with their comments and insights. I am overwhelmed with gratitude to the many men and women who have given me the privilege of accompanying them as they developed their friendship with God. Some of them have given me permission to use their experiences here to illustrate how friendship changes the real world. The trust I have been given by those who seek spiritual direction continues to bring me to my knees.

For the past thirteen years, I have codirected a program (called tertianship) for priests and brothers of the Society of Jesus in preparation for their final vows. They have come from many parts of the world, and each year, they have made the Spiritual Exercises of St. Ignatius of Loyola for thirty days at Eastern Point Retreat House in Gloucester, Massachusetts. I've been privileged to listen to their experiences of developing a deeper friendship with Jesus—an experience that has impelled them out into the wider world to make their mark in cooperation with their friend. The experience has been enriching for me, and I am immensely grateful to these men, to the staff at Eastern Point Retreat House who help make it a "thin place," and to my superiors who have given me this profound work to do.

Also for the past thirteen years, I have lived at Campion Center, a building that formerly housed large numbers of young Jesuits studying philosophy and theology in preparation for ordination to the priesthood. Now half of the building contains the Michael G. Pierce, SJ, Pavilion for elderly and sick Jesuits of the New England province; the other half is a renewal center. I live with a wonderful community of Jesuits; many of us are here for our final days before burial in the province cemetery next to the building. It is a great gift to live with my brothers as we all face old age, illness, and death with a spirit of hope, good humor, and deep faith in Jesus, who has called each to be his companion and friend. You might expect gloom here, but you would not find it. Friendship with Jesus seems to be making us better images of God as we age. I say this of my brothers—I am not so sure of myself. But they certainly have encouraged me with their interest in what I am doing, their words of congratulations and helpful suggestions after homilies, and their companionship. I am immensely grateful to be a member of this community of friends in the Lord.

I want to thank all those who have taken the time to write to thank me, to encourage me, or to make suggestions as a result of reading previous books. Writers send words out into the world in the hope that they will reach someone and have an impact. I have been blessed with this gift and with readers who take the time to respond. Know that I am grateful to all of you who read this book. If you get to the penultimate page, you will see how I pray for all of you. Many thanks!

Finally, my deepest debt of gratitude is to the Friend who created me, gave me the parents and sisters, teachers, mentors and friends who have nurtured me over this long life of eighty years. *Laus Deo semper!*

Friendship with God in the Real World

See, I am making all things new.
—REVELATION 21:5

God wants our friendship. Does this statement seem idealistic and otherworldly? To be in touch with God, do you need to get out of touch with the hurly-burly of ordinary life? Retreat houses are usually located in rural areas and have large, private grounds so that you can pray undisturbed. At these retreat houses, near the end of a retreat, retreat directors and those making retreats often speak of returning to the "real world," and they sound regretful. Closeness to God seems to require distance from the world.

Much of a Christian's religious teaching invites a separation of religion from ordinary life. Heaven is often presented as a place to which we go when we die, and it is contrasted with this dark and evil world. Church on Sunday becomes a refuge from real life, to which we are forced to return on

Monday. For centuries in the Roman Catholic Church, religious life was presented as a retreat from the world to a higher calling; marriage and raising a family and working at a "regular" job seemed to be on a lower rung in the hierarchy of religious values. People easily came to the conclusion that, in some ways, God and the world were in opposition.

In addition, many who are active in the world look with suspicion, even disdain, on religious people who try to give moral or political advice. "Religion has no place and no relevance in the public square," they say. "Your advice is all well and good, but in the real world, it won't work. You people stick to your prayers and leave the rough-and-tumble of politics and business to us practical people." Does closeness to God really mean we must keep our distance from "unreligious" life?

God Has a Dream for This World

In the liturgy of Advent, we hear the great prophecies of the Hebrew Bible. These prophecies, most of them from Isaiah, tell us about God's dream for our world and for our world *now*. In other words, they do not just foretell what will happen; they proclaim, first and foremost, what God intends and hopes for creation itself. Moreover, the prophesies aim to encourage a discouraged and desperate people to live toward the fulfillment of this dream, to continue to be the light of the world as God's people.

In Isaiah, God says: "They shall beat their swords into plowshares, / and their spears into pruning hooks; / nation shall not lift up sword against nation, / neither shall they learn war any more" (Isaiah 2:4). "The wolf shall live with the lamb, / the leopard shall lie down with the kid. . . . They will not hurt or destroy / on all my holy mountain; / for the earth will be full of the knowledge of the LORD as the waters cover the sea" (Isaiah 11:6–9). Rather than see these prophecies as promises about a distant future, think of them as indications of what God wants for our created world now and always. These prophecies express God's dream in creating our world.

God wants a world in which human beings work together in harmony and friendship with God, with one another, and with all of creation. We are God's children, created in God's image and likeness, and asked to help God fulfill the dream for this created world. Sometimes I use the image of God as a parent inviting adult children to join the family business. The world is God's family business. Only in this world can God attain the dream. But God can attain that dream only if we, who are created in God's image and likeness, live out our likeness as God's sons and daughters and accept the invitation to join the family business.

The whole of creation, of course, is made in the image and likeness of God—God is the only reality, the only model for creation. However, we humans are distinct in that we are created to be like God in our self-consciousness, in our thinking, feeling, and acting. Because we act not just from instinct but also from intention, we are created to act in harmony with God's intention for the world. That's the awesome and exhilarating challenge of being human, because, like God, we must choose how to act. We can choose to act in harmony—or out of harmony—with God's dream.

Christians believe that Jesus of Nazareth is God incarnate, in human flesh. It looks as though God, seeing how badly we mishandled our role in this created world, decided to show how a human being should act as one made in God's image. Jesus grew into an adult friend of his Abba, his "dear Father," and participated in God's dream for the world in the way God intends all human beings to cooperate. At the Last Supper, Jesus said to his disciples, and therefore to all of us adult followers:

> You are my friends if you do what I command you. I do not call you servants any longer, because the servant does not know what the master is doing; but I have called you friends, because I have made known to you everything that I have heard from my Father. You did not choose me but I chose you. And I appointed you to go and bear fruit, fruit that will last, so that the Father will give you whatever you ask him in my name. I am giving you these commands so that you may love one another. (John 15:14–17)

After the resurrection, Jesus returned to the upper room and said, "Peace be with you. As the Father has sent me, so I send you," and he breathed on them, thus indicating that he was giving them the breath, or spirit, of God (John 20:21–22); this made it possible for them to develop fully into adult friends of God and to participate in God's life here in the world.

John sets up this scene in the upper room as a new or renewed creation story. We, who at the first creation were created to be the image bearers of God by the breath or spirit of God, now receive that Spirit in a new and even more intimate way so that we can be who we are created to be, images of God, friends of God, other Christs in this world, which so desperately needs such friends of God.

What Are the Practical Consequences of Living as Friends of God?

If what I have been saying is true—and Christians profess that it is—then this spirituality of friendship with God is the purpose for which God created us. We are created to become friends of God and to cooperate with God to develop a world in which the wolf does live with the lamb, in which swords are beaten into ploughshares, in which all God's children live in peace. Every one of us adults is invited to become a friend of God and a prophet (Wisdom 7:27). Jesus calls each of us Christians his friends and sends us out into this world in the same way he was sent. Each of us is called to follow Jesus, not to imitate him slavishly but to discern what our role in God's work is to be and how we are to live out our vocation as God-images and adult friends of God in our time and place and circumstances. We can choose to sit out the call, but if we do so, we become part of the world's problem, not part of the solution.

What does it mean, then, to be a friend of God, an image bearer of God, another Christ? The rest of this book attempts to answer that question.

God, in Whose Image
We Are Made

I am the LORD *your God. [Y]ou shall*
have no other gods before me.
—EXODUS 20:2–3

The first letter of John states, "In this is love, not that we loved God but that he loved us and sent his Son to be the atoning sacrifice for our sins. . . . We love because he first loved us" (1 John 4:10, 19). When we love someone or something, we are attracted to what already exists. But we exist because of God's love. We do not exist for God to be attracted to us; rather, God's desire for us creates us and makes us attractive—to God! God's love is not contingent on anything we are or do. Nor is God's love utilitarian—that is, God does not love us to achieve some other purpose, for instance, to convert some other person or to achieve a goal in God's scheme for the world. Before we ever became aware of God, we were already the focus of God's love. Also, nothing we do or say changes God's love for us. Through sin we alienate ourselves from God, but God still loves us and pursues our friendship.

We are made in God's image. And the God in whose image we are made is absolute love, given and not deserved.

Assess Your Perception of God

Perceiving God as absolute love is a hard lesson for us to learn because we are so conditioned to love with ifs and buts attached: "I will love you if you are a good boy"; "I love you because you are so beautiful"; "I will love you as long as you are faithful to me"; "If you loved me, you would . . ." God is not, however, like King Lear in Shakespeare's play, who demands to know how much his three daughters love him before dividing his kingdom among them. When Cordelia, the one he loves most and who loves him gratuitously, cannot come up with words to match the flattery of her sisters, Lear disowns her and banishes her from his sight forever. Many of us tend to imagine God as being like Lear, testing us to see whether we are worthy of love. But that's not the truth about God, as the first letter of John points out. God loves us first, and without conditions.

When we realize that we are attracted to God and want closeness to God, we are like a young man or woman who is attracted to someone else. Can you recall a time when you were attracted to someone but were not sure that the other person was attracted to you? I remember times like that. What a surge of joy when I found out that the other person was just as attracted to me! It seemed like a miracle; I found it difficult to contain my happiness. Well, that's just a pale comparison to what we experience in our growing love for God. We could say that God is hopelessly in love with us from the get-go. In fact, that love is the great energy that creates us. Experiencing even a taste of God's love for you can make you very happy indeed. And, as we shall see in chapter 4, happy people have an effect on the world.

There's something else we need to know: God is neither coercive nor violent. God can have friendship with us only if we willingly accept the offer. In creating human beings, God has tied his own hands, so to speak, and become vulnerable—vulnerable to our rejection, our lack of response. This idea flies in the face of the way God is often depicted in Scripture and in religious discourse. We hear that God is a God of power and might.

There is a strand of the Scriptures that would lead us to see God as using coercion and violence against disobedient people. Some sections of the Old Testament seem to sanction ethnic cleansing as God's way of ensuring that the people remain true to the covenant they have with God. Other passages show God as vengeful and violent against those who refuse to obey the law. But I would urge you to take the long view both of Scripture and of tradition as you ponder the Mystery who is God.

The Old Testament also shows God as endlessly forgiving and merciful and as willing almost to grovel before his people to bring them back to their senses (Micah 6:3). Finally, a sustained contemplation of the life and death of Jesus of Nazareth raises questions about the ambiguity of Scripture and gives us permission to see the portrayal of God as violent as a sign of our own ambivalence about God and about our own use of power. For one thing, Jesus never uses coercion to attain his purposes. Even his healing power can be accessed only by those who are willing to receive it. He often says to those who have been cured, "Your faith has made you well" (Mark 5:34). In his hometown of Nazareth, he could do little healing because of the people's lack of faith; he seems perplexed at their unbelief (see Mark 6:1–6). He was the Messiah, the anointed one, promised by God to bring about restoration of God's dream for the world, yet he refused the devil's temptations to use his powers in coercive ways to prove his credentials.

And if ever God had reason to react in violence, it was at Golgotha. We Christians believe that Jesus is God Incarnate. He is God's response to the mess we have made of the good world God created. Yet we delivered him to a cruel and tortured death. God did not respond with anger and violence but with forgiveness and resurrection. In light of the life and death of Jesus, the God in whose image we are created cannot be said to be violent.

Dare to Contemplate God's Love

Ignatius of Loyola must have experienced the immense joy and happiness of realizing that God had always loved him passionately and without reservation, even while he was doing everything in his power to keep God at a proper distance or to drive God away. Ignatius had not sought God for most of his early life, but when he awakened to his desire for God, he found that God had been seeking him all his life. His heart overflowed with love and affection for God and with a desire to join God's loving action in the world. At the end of his *Spiritual Exercises*, Ignatius proposes a contemplation for attaining love to help those who have made these Exercises come to the kind of love for God that Ignatius had experienced. I suggest that you take some time, before going ahead with the reading of this book, to do this contemplation.[1]

Before you begin, let me say something about the word *contemplation*. For Ignatius, contemplation was a rather simple exercise, one in which we allow our heart, mind, senses, and imagination free rein so that God can use them to reveal something about Godself to us. It is a way to forget our concerns and ourselves so that God can get a word in edgewise. You are contemplative when you pay attention to the play of sunlight on snow, for example; as you do, you forget the pain in your back or the concern about your bank account, and God has a chance to break through to reveal something important to you. You can also read a passage of Scripture and let it capture your imagination the way a novel or a poem might. The process of paying attention to something besides your own concerns and worries gives God a chance to communicate. That's what Ignatius meant by contemplation. Just recently, for example, a woman read aloud the words of Isaiah 43:4, "You are precious in my sight, / and honored, and I love you," and found herself unaccountably sobbing with relief, joy, and desire for God; her reactions surprised her. She had paid attention to those words, and something unexpected happened.

So when Ignatius calls this exercise Contemplation for Attaining Love and then gives four points, he does not intend for us to spend the time of prayer merely thinking about those points. He wants us to *experience* the world in that way. So if you want to engage in the exercise, I invite you to use all your senses, your mind, your imagination, your emotions, and your memory; if you enjoy the outdoors, go outside and walk or sit or play; if you enjoy music, listen to it or play it; if you like to paint or use clay or any other medium, go ahead. The main thing is that you are asking to experience how much God has loved and cherished you so that you will grow in your own love for God.

Ignatius makes two preliminary points: first, love is shown more in deeds than in words, and second, love desires mutuality. The first is rather easy to understand, but the second can take your breath away when you realize that the One who wants something from us in mutuality is the Creator of the universe—the one who needs nothing. Yet without our acceptance of the love God offers, God is helpless; under those circumstances, God is a lover who seems to love in vain. Let that thought sink in. Doesn't it boggle the mind?

▪A Contemplation to Attain Love

Remember that God is looking at you, waiting for you to pay attention. Even that thought can knock you over. The Creator of the universe is looking at *you*, waiting for you to pay attention. Then tell God what you want, namely to have a deeply felt knowledge of how good God is and has been to you so that you will want to love God in return *(S.E. No. 233)*.

First (S.E. No. 234) allow your memory to recall all the gifts you have received in life.

Ignatius mentions the gifts of "creation, redemption, and particular gifts." Let the memories roll. Ignatius suggests "pondering with great affection how much God our Lord has done for me, and how much He has given me of what He has; and further, how according to His divine plan, it is the Lord's wish, as far as He is able, to give me Himself." God wants you to exist in this world and has done everything to make that possible; also, God wants to give you Godself "as far as He is able." Let that sink in. How do you react? Tell God what's in your mind and heart. Give yourself some time with this exercise. Don't rush to the next point.

In his second point (S.E. No. 235), Ignatius invites us to "see how God dwells in creatures."

Everything that exists is an image of God; God dwells in everything. So pay attention to rocks, flowers, birds, dumps, trees, deer, and other human beings. As you pay attention, do you feel a sense of awe, a sense of divine presence? God dwells in everything, including you and me. Again, take time with this exercise and tell God what's in your mind and heart.

In the third point (S.E. No. 236), Ignatius invites us to "consider how God works and labors on my behalf in all the created things on the face of the earth."

God is acting always in everything to bring about the kind of world God wants for you and for all of humanity and for the whole of creation. How do you react as you allow yourself to imagine this whole world as a place where God is working for your good and the good of the whole? Tell God what is in your mind and heart.

In the fourth point (S.E. No. 237), Ignatius suggests that we "see how all that is good and every gift descends from on high . . . as rays descend from the sun, waters from a fountain."

You might spend time outside on a sunny day, seeing the sunlight illuminating everything, feeling its warmth on your body, and imagining how God is creating and bathing you in love. Again, tell God what's in your mind and heart.

This kind of contemplation can lead us to want to love God with our whole mind and heart and soul, to become the friend God wants us to be. Ignatius suggests a prayer that may express what you want to say to God.

Take, Lord, and receive all my liberty,
my memory,
my understanding,
and my entire will,
all that I have and possess.
You gave it all to me;
to you, Lord, I give it all back.
All is yours,
dispose of it entirely according to your will.
Give me the grace to love you,
for that is enough for me.
(S.E. No. 234)

What a radical prayer! You may not be able to say it with your whole heart and mind right away. If you find it too much, ask God to help you be able to say it and mean it. When you get right down to it, this prayer is only an expression of the truth of things, namely that we are all creatures who have everything by gift from God's creative hand and heart. It is an expression of the first commandment, affirming that God alone is God and everything else depends on God's creative desire at every moment. But this truth is not at all easy for us to live out. So as we say this prayer, we might add the words of the father of the demon-possessed boy: "I believe; help my unbelief" (Mark 9:24). Love and faith go hand in hand, and they are both gifts to be prayed for continually. ∷

✠ 3

Our Role in the World as It Is

God saw everything that he had made,
and . . . it was very good.

—GENESIS 1:31

The Contemplation for Attaining Love can help us realize at a deep level that God does love us first and has only
our good in mind. And as we grow into contemplating our
world this way, we recognize more and more that every
place and situation is holy ground because God is present
and working there. Gerard Manley Hopkins, who every
year of his Jesuit life made this contemplation at least once,
distilled the experience in the poem "God's Grandeur."

The world is charged with the grandeur of God.
    It will flame out, like shining from shook foil;
    It gathers to a greatness, like the ooze of oil

> Crushed. Why do men then now not reck
>   his rod?
> Generations have trod, have trod, have trod;
>   And all is seared with trade; bleared, smeared
>   with toil;
>   And wears man's smudge and shares man's
>   smell: the soil
> Is bare now, nor can foot feel, being shod.
>
> And, for all this, nature is never spent;
>   There lives the dearest freshness deep down
>   things;
> And though the last lights off the black West went
>   Oh, morning, at the brown brink eastwards,
>   springs—
> Because the Holy Ghost over the bent
>   World broods with warm breast and with ah!
>   bright wings.[2]

Hopkins sees how bleak and hard the world can be, but at the same time, he experiences God's loving presence lighting it up. The last lines evoke the image of the Holy Spirit as a bird sitting on the egg that is the world, not only bent because eggs are round but also bent with human folly and sin. It is a very hopeful image indeed.

The World Is God's, Whether or Not We Believe It

Just as we need to be clear about who God is as we reflect on what friendship with God in the world entails, so too we need to be clear about the world as it really is. Many Christians have a distorted view of the "world." For many, it is a place in which we are tested to see whether we are worthy of going to heaven when we die. For others, the world is an evil place. Yet our faith tells us that God, who is Father, Word, and Spirit, created this vast, complex universe out of nothing, with pure generosity, and saw that "it was very good" (Genesis 1:31). Our faith also affirms that God creates this vast universe intentionally; that is, God has a purpose in creation.

I believe that God's intention for our world can be summed up in this way: God wants a world where we human beings live in harmony and friendship with God, with one another, and with the rest of creation, cooperating with God wherever we are.

God is always creating and sustaining this universe, always at work in it to move it toward the end for which it is created. Hence, we encounter God as present, indwelling, and active in everything that exists at every moment of our existence. And exercises such as the Contemplation for Attaining Love give us a chance to experience that encounter and to rejoice in it. So in this world we meet the living God who is always trying to draw each of us into harmony with the divine intention.

The world is what it is independent of our beliefs. When she was questioning God's existence, the British theologian Frances Young "heard" these words: "It makes no difference to me whether you believe in me or not."[3] She found it immensely consoling and freeing to realize that God's existence did not depend on her belief. Well, the reality of our world as created and sustained and, in Jesus, inhabited by God does not depend on our belief. It just *is*, at every moment of its existence, dependent on God's creative, sustaining, and redeeming desire. Human beings are created for friendship with God, with one another, and with the whole created universe independent of who believes this.

Whether or not we believe, our hearts are restless until they rest in God. And in this universe, the Son of God became a human being, lived, died, and was raised from the dead. Our world and everyone in it—independent of anyone's belief—have physical ties with the risen Jesus and are different because of his existence. And whether or not we believe it, the spirit of God has been poured out into the hearts and minds of human beings and influences them to act as sons and daughters of God, wherever they are in the world.

In other words, God is always at work to bring about the divine dream, the kingdom or rule of God—whether or not we believe it.

The World Is Both Old and New

But we human beings have not lived in harmony with the divine intention. To explain the sorry state of the world, the third chapter of Genesis tells the story of the man and woman eating the fruit from the tree of the knowledge of good and evil. According to the story, by God's generous gift alone, the man and the woman were like God and would live forever as God's friends. The tempter, however, insinuated that God did not want them to eat this fruit because then they would be like God. God is not a rival of anyone or anything, but, insanely, the man and woman disobey God to become like God—and thus they become less like God, distorted images of God. Because of their folly, alienation from God and from God's intention for us entered our world and ruined the dream.

Still, God has not given up on the dream. God chose a people, the Jews, to keep alive belief in the one true God and hope for the world, which is now broken and alienated. The prophets, such as the one known as Third Isaiah, articulated that hope as a promise to create a new heavens and a new earth.

For I am about to create new heavens
    and a new earth;
the former things shall not be remembered
    or come to mind.
But be glad and rejoice forever
    in what I am creating;
for I am about to create Jerusalem as a joy,
    and its people as a delight.
I will rejoice in Jerusalem,
    and delight in my people;
no more shall the sound of weeping be heard in it,
    or the cry of distress.
No more shall there be in it
    an infant that lives but a few days,
    or an old person who does not live out a
        lifetime;
for one who dies at a hundred years will be
        considered a youth,
    and one who falls short of a hundred will be
        considered accursed.
They shall build houses and inhabit them;
    they shall plant vineyards and eat their fruit.
(Isaiah 65:17–21)

The prophet delivered these words to the Israelites, who had returned from exile in Babylon. They were experiencing the difficulties of rebuilding their lives and their religious practices in a land that was alien to them, a land most of them had never seen. Often in the Bible we find such promises of what God wants to do and will do, and often they are delivered at dark times in the history of the Israelites. Jews and Christians believe that the new heavens and the new earth have to do with this world, not with a world of heavenly spirits alone. Somehow God will make this world new.

For many Jews in Jesus' time, this belief in God's promise of a new heavens and a new earth meant belief in the bodily resurrection of the dead, which would come to pass with the arrival of the Messiah at the end of history. Christians believe that the Messiah has come in Jesus of Nazareth and that within history God has already resurrected him. Thus, we believe that by raising Jesus bodily from the dead, God has already begun the new heavens and new earth. And because Jesus has a body with ties to the whole universe, in some mysterious way, the new heavens and new earth are transforming our world right now. We, who still live in the "old earth," are invited to live now as citizens of that "new earth." This is what friendship with God in Christ Jesus entails.

But our world is not totally transformed. We still feel the effects of original sin, of alienation from God, and we continually have to struggle with the pulls of that old earth in which we are enmeshed. Hence, nothing we do, even our holiest action, is totally free from the effects of the old earth. Those effects color our motivations, our attitudes, and our behaviors. It is good to remember this as we try to do our best to live as citizens of the new heavens and the new earth.

Living in Two Worlds Requires Discernment

Because we live simultaneously in two worlds (which are really one world in the process of redemption), we need to become discerning. We are the products of a world that is simultaneously alienated from God and, in Jesus, united with God. We constantly hear siren calls that want to pull us back to the old earth. That world exerts a mighty pull because we are part of it in every fiber of our being. Jesus himself became part of it, which is why he was vulnerable to temptation, just as we are. If we are moved to treat those who oppose us with kindness and courtesy, we will be tempted to think that we are being weak and cowardly. If we sense an urge to speak out against something unjust or immoral, we might have the thought, *But others who are good people don't seem to be bothered*. The values of the two worlds we live in are at odds, and unfortunately, the loudest voice often is that of the world alienated from God.

In addition, another voice tries to keep us from developing our friendship with God, namely the Father of Lies, the one Jesus called the Satan. It is not fashionable to speak of the devil these days, but that fashion may be the best strategy the devil has devised. At least that is what C. S. Lewis suggested in his humorous but deadly serious *The Screwtape*

Letters. The letters purport to be written by a senior devil to his nephew, giving him instruction on how to tempt human beings. In the preface, Lewis writes:

> There are two equal and opposite errors into which our race can fall about the devils. One is to disbelieve in their existence. The other is to believe, and to feel an excessive and unhealthy interest in them. They themselves are equally pleased by both errors, and hail a materialist or a magician with the same delight.[4]

Jesus surely believed in the existence of the one he called the Satan, but he did not show an excessive interest in Satan, and the same is true for saints throughout the centuries.

Friendship Changes Both Heart and Mind

In a series of lectures for BBC Radio in 1930 and 1932, the Scottish philosopher John Macmurray spoke of the dangerous situation into which the Western world had fallen as a result of the Enlightenment. He rightly extolled the development of the intellect that the Enlightenment had fostered, a development that led to great scientific and technological breakthroughs, modern methods of historical and literary criticism, and the growth of democratic governments. But there was a downside, he noted, in that there had not been a comparable development of the human heart, of human affectivity, to match our intellectual development. "As a result," he said:

> we are intellectually civilized and emotionally primitive; and we have reached the point at which the development of knowledge threatens to destroy us. Knowledge is power, but emotion is the master of our values and of the uses, therefore, to which we put our power. Emotionally we are primitive, childish, undeveloped. Therefore, we have the tastes, the appetites, the interests and apprehensions of children. But we have in our hands a vast set of powers, which are the products of our intellectual development. We have used these powers to construct an intricate machinery of life, all in the service of our childish desires. And now we are waking up to the fact that we cannot control it; that we do not even know what we want to do with it. So we are beginning to be afraid of the work of our hands. That is the modern dilemma.[5]

Do you sense, as I do, that he is talking about our present world even though the lectures were delivered before the outbreak of World War II, the horrors of Hitler's "final solution," the atomic bomb, and all the other horrors our world has seen since that time? We do not seem to have advanced much beyond the primitive, childish emotional development Macmurray diagnosed at that time, nor are we less afraid of what we are capable of doing with the work of our hands. How do we develop emotionally into the maturity that will allow us to use the power our intellects have put into our hands for the good of our world rather than its destruction? In the terms of this book, how do we become the kind of adult friends God needs to bring about the new heavens and the new earth?

Macmurray believed that "emotion is the master of our values and of the uses . . . to which we put our power." So the answer to our question is not a matter of getting our ideas or our values straight through disciplined thinking. Disciplined thinking alone is what got us into this predicament. We need to develop a discipline of the heart, and this is precisely what engaging in friendship with God can do.

We Grow into Emotional Maturity

When we engage in any friendship, our hearts are changed, often without our noticing what has happened. The closer I become to a friend, the more both of us reveal of our true selves. Some of what I reveal is not pretty, but I find that my friend remains my friend in spite of my shabbiness, my narrow-mindedness, my bouts of anger and moodiness. As a result, I am changed, and for the better. I find that I do not have to be so defensive with this friend, with other friends, and with others I meet. I become more confident and unafraid with people and, in the process, become less shabby, less narrow-minded, and less prone to bouts of anger or moodiness. And others become less edgy and on alert when they're around me. As friendship changes my heart, I become emotionally more mature and better able to use what power I have for the good of others and not just to protect myself.

The same thing happens, and with greater effect, in our friendship with God. As I engage in friendship with God, I find that God loves me warts and all, and I am more and more willing to face my dark moods and sinful tendencies with God. Not only that, but I also begin to ask God for help in overcoming these tendencies, to make me more like Jesus. God's friendship helps me face the truth about myself in a way that leads to a more honest relationship with others as well. I regret hurting others and so ask for forgiveness and make amends. In my relationship with God, I reveal more and more of myself and become freer of the hang-ups and neuroses that bedevil my other relationships at home and at work. I talk with God about my life at home and at work and find that this kind of conversation helps me bring harmony and productivity to both places. Simply put, engaging in the friendship with God transforms me, and through me—and, of course, through those around me—a small part of the world changes for the better.

The discipline of the heart that leads to its transformation, however, will come about only if we pay attention to what goes in our interior life. As we go about our daily lives trying to live as adult friends of God, different voices pull us—some from God, some from our alienated world, some from our own psychological baggage, and some from the Satan. How do we decide which attractions and inclinations are from God? In the history of spirituality, the way to answer this question has been called discernment of spirits. What this term means is that we pay attention to our inner states as we go through life. Why? Because from our inner states come the good and evil that we do (see Matthew 15:18–20). We can learn how to discern the spirits, those inner voices or movements, but we need the help of others to learn how to do so. I have written a short introduction to this process in *A Friendship Like No Other: Experiencing God's Amazing Embrace*. But I want to say something here because it bears on how we grow toward emotional maturity and, therefore, on how we live in this real world.[6]

We Learn the Discernment of Spirits

One thing is clear: we cannot discern the spirits if we are not aware of them. To become a discerning friend of God, we need to grow in awareness of what goes on inside us. In a book on Greek Orthodox spirituality, *The Mountain of Silence*, Kyriacos Markides asks Elder Father Maximos whether, according to Orthodox spirituality, the heart is "the depository where what Freud called 'repression' takes place." Maximos replies: "What you called 'repression' is totally unacceptable in real spiritual medicine. . . . In the spiritual arena . . . we aim at the transmutation or metamorphosis of our passions, not the actual storing of them into the so-called subconscious." Later he continued: "According to the spirituality of the holy elders, the subconscious must never remain dark. The aim is to purify it, distill it, and make it transparent. We must never repress our weaknesses and passions. The aim of the *Ecclesia* (the church) as a method of healing is to sanctify the human individual, the whole person."[7]

Elder Maximos hits the target. For too long in the history of Western Christian spirituality, repression of unwanted feelings, impulses, thoughts, and desires was taught as the preferred method toward spiritual growth. But God wants to heal us through and through. To allow God to do this, we must be willing to face our darkest and most troubling impulses in God's healing presence. The psalmist who uttered the terrifying words, "Happy shall they be who take your little ones / and dash them against the rock!" (Psalm 137:9) could be healed of his murderous rage against the Babylonians only by letting God know that he felt this way. (It would be comforting to know that, after voicing those sentiments, he later asked God to heal him of this rage.)

As we try to figure out how to act in this world that is simultaneously the old world and the new world, we need to pay attention to everything important that goes through our hearts and minds so that we can discern how to act in tune with God's dream for the world. The only way forward for God's dream is for more and more of us friends to learn how to discern in this way.

Please understand that such cooperation cannot be had by blind obedience to authority. It can come only from adults who take seriously their God-given opportunity to try to live as much as possible as citizens of the new earth inaugurated by the resurrection of Jesus from the dead and the outpouring of his Spirit. Our cooperation with God will be the result of our ongoing efforts to distinguish the movements of our hearts and minds that come from God from those that come from old-world thinking or from the Satan.

Of course, we don't experience friendship with God in isolation; this holy friendship is designed for community, and it requires community, the church, for it to flourish. The church as the people of God is the bearer of the tradition that goes back centuries, and that tradition informs the consciences of the individuals in the church. So friends of God do not cavalierly dismiss significant aspects of that tradition as outmoded by modern knowledge. Those of us who have developed our friendship with God will see the tradition and authority of the church as a living source of wisdom. At the same time, friendship with God frees us from servile obedience to tradition and authority in the church and enables us to see this tradition as a living one to which we are called to contribute. We make our contribution by trying to discern how to speak and act in daily life as "friends of God, and prophets" (Wisdom 7:27).

Thus, all of us in the church need to pay attention to our tradition and to what authorities in the church tell us;

we find God in and through our membership in the church, and that church has a duty to teach with authority. But the new heavens and the new earth require more and more adult children of God who take seriously their own call to make a significant contribution to God's family business—through attention to their own friendship with God as it works itself out in real life. No one else can do in God's world what I am called to do in my small patch. God depends on each of us to bring about the full flowering of the new heavens and new earth that Jesus inaugurated. God depends on the willingness of each of us to engage honestly in the friendship and to submit to the discipline of the heart that it entails—another example of God's vulnerability!

I know that I have only touched the surface of how discernment will help us figure out how to live as citizens in our workplaces, our countries, and our world. In the notes here, you will find resources for more on this topic. But I cannot end this section without saying as strongly as I can that the future of our world depends on all of us. God cannot achieve the dream without our adult cooperation. And we cannot become adults without allowing our friendship with God to help us grow into emotional adults whose desires correspond with what God desires. How we live and act is immensely important to God. Say that to yourself: "How I live and act in this world is immensely important to God." Let it sink in, and follow through.[8]

▪ 4

Inner Life,
Public Life

They are in the world.

—JOHN 17:11

This book is about our friendship with God and the impact this friendship has on the world as it is. But we start with the fact that God's prior love for us already affects the world; after all, God's love is what creates the world. Too often we act as though God were off in heaven apart from this universe, this planet, and our lives. But if you contemplated the world with Ignatius of Loyola, using the exercise at the end of chapter 2, you know—with heart knowledge—that God is always active in this world, always creating it, always sustaining it, always laboring in it, always present to it. "The world is charged with the grandeur of God."

But God also affects the world through friendship with *you*.

We Cannot Separate Inward from Outward

We suffer from the persistent illusion that we can separate our inner lives from our public lives, as though one had nothing to do with the other. For example, as long as I do not act on my hatred for you, no one is the wiser and no one is hurt.

I started writing this chapter on February 10, 2009. In that day's edition of the *Boston Globe*, the comic strip *Zits*, by Jerry Scott and Jim Borgman, illustrated this inner-outer concept very well. In the first panel, Jeremy Duncan, the teenage son, is seen walking toward his parents, who are on a couch reading; behind him is a dark mass. In the second panel, he is behind the couch near his father, and the dark mass covers part of the panel behind him; his parents look up surprised. The dark mass covers the whole third panel, with only the eyes of the parents visible. The father says, "Somebody's in a dark mood." To which his wife says, "Ya think?"

Reflect for a few moments on encounters you've had with people who were in a sour mood, or recall a recent encounter when you were the moody one. I live in a rather large Jesuit community. On any given day, there might be one or two in the community in a bad mood, and I might be one of them. What happens at lunch or dinner when I sit down at the table in such a mood? An uneasiness settles in the atmosphere and on the conversation. Everyone knows that Bill is in a bad mood, and no one wants to say the wrong thing that might make it worse. No one feels at ease, and no one feels comfortable enough to bring up the elephant at the table. Now imagine yourself at lunch with six people, two of whom have just had a bitter argument. Everybody is affected, right? So it's an illusion to think that our inner states have no effect on public life.

Jesus knew the good and baleful effects of inner attitudes, as noted in Luke's Sermon on the Plain.

> No good tree bears bad fruit, nor again does a bad tree bear good fruit; for each tree is known by its own fruit. Figs are not gathered from thorns, nor are grapes picked from a bramble bush. The good person out of the good treasure of the heart produces good, and the evil person out of evil treasure produces evil; for it is out of the abundance of the heart that the mouth speaks. (Luke 6:43–45)

A Healthy Soul Brings Good Results

Jesus is a clear example of a friend of God who has changed our world. But think of the effect of his early friends and followers. The Acts of the Apostles provides one example, perhaps idealized, but nonetheless indicative of how they tried to live and how their life together affected others.

> Now the whole group of those who believed were of one heart and soul, and no one claimed private ownership of any possessions, but everything they owned was held in

common. With great power the apostles gave their testimony to the resurrection of the Lord Jesus, and great
grace was upon them all. There was not a needy person
among them, for as many as owned lands or houses sold
them and brought the proceeds of what was sold. They
laid it at the apostles' feet, and it was distributed to each
as any had need. There was a Levite, a native of Cyprus,
Joseph, to whom the apostles gave the name Barnabas
(which means "son of encouragement"). He sold a field
that belonged to him, then brought the money, and laid
it at the apostles' feet. (Acts 4:32–37)

Christians grew in numbers rapidly throughout the
Mediterranean world, and according to Rodney Stark,
author of *The Rise of Christianity*, one of the main reasons
was their genuine love and care for one another and for
their neighbors.[9] As a result, Christians and their neighbors weathered the frequent plagues that decimated the
cities of that world better than people who avoided caring for others. Thus, people's friendship with God changed
the known world of that time—and it was a harsh, brutal world. What would our world be without the effect of
St. Benedict and his sister St. Scholastica and their monastic
followers, who are credited with saving the manuscripts of
Greek and Roman civilization from almost-certain extinc-
tion and whose monasteries still grace the world! Or without the effect of St. Francis and St. Clare of Assisi through

the millions of Franciscans who have touched the lives of so many people over the past eight hundred years!

But people who remain relatively unknown have changed some part of our world because of their closeness to God. Take, for example, a man I know who told me of how friendship with Jesus changed his attitude during the recession of 2008. He and his wife have two young children. One night he could not sleep because of worry about what the recession was doing to the family's savings for his children's education and his and his wife's retirement. Tossing and turning and finding no relief, he finally began to say the name of Jesus in prayer. Gradually, a peace descended on him, and he fell asleep. The next day, he went to work as a helping professional with peace of heart. His financial picture had not changed, but he had, and that change had an effect on his dealings with his family, his coworkers, and those whom he serves.

Think of the thousands of African American followers of Rev. Martin Luther King Jr., who paved the way for the sweeping changes in the way African Americans were treated in the United States. They were motivated by their friendship with Jesus to confront racist laws in a nonviolent way that transformed this country. Their resolve brought about the conversion of many white Americans to the civil rights cause and drew the attention of people all over the world. In 2008, the people of the United States elected an African American as president, something that could not have happened without the courageous actions of those earlier citizens.

In an article in *America* magazine, Barbara Kouba recounts her bout, at age seventeen, with a rare blood disease that resulted in her hospitalization in a ward with children suffering from terrible illnesses. She began to hate God, eventually saying, "I will not love you, God. You're a monstrous sadist." After medication brought healing, she fell into a deep depression. She was treated with medication, shock therapy, and psychotherapy, but nothing helped. Finally, she ended up in a psychiatric hospital. One evening she asked to be locked in the Quiet Room, where she huddled in a corner. A message came through to her: "I love you. I'm proud of you." She knew it was God, and she responded, "I hate you." God said, "I love you for hating me." Later in the conversation, God said, "I love you and am proud that you would never believe in anyone you think could be cruel or sadistic. I want suffering to end." When this night was over, Kouba was a different person, and within a week she was released from the hospital. Since that time she has spent her life helping others.[10]

Garson Kanin recounts some of his visits to Felix Frankfurter, the famous justice of the Supreme Court. One day Frankfurter said:

> I have had a serious experience here. . . . You saw that nurse who went out a while ago? The tall, pretty, blond one? Audrée? We've been spending many hours here

together, and I've had an opportunity to find out a great deal about her life. She is a devout Catholic. Look here. I have spent a good deal of energy attempting to avoid prejudice. But the dogma of the Catholic Church, or of any other denomination for that matter, has always put me off. Now this girl, this Audrée—I have never known generosity of such quality, or such rare kindness. Oh yes, far, far beyond duty. Overwhelming courtesy. And I have been asking questions, delving into the matter, trying to discover the wellspring of such superior behavior. Do you know what it turns out to be? Can you guess? Simply this: a practical application of her Catholicism. I've never known anyone who practiced a religion, whose everyday life is based upon a religion as much as this girl's is.[11]

Perhaps you will be reminded of someone whose "practiced religion" has had a profound impact on the world you live in. You might recall someone who has changed your life because of his or her relationship with God. It could be your mother or father, a neighbor, a teacher, a nurse, the local bus driver, or the person who delivers your mail. You have been touched, as I have been, by people who acted toward you in a certain way because of their friendship with God. Friendship with God has an effect on this enormous, wounded world—one person at a time.

If you know any alcoholics or drug addicts in recovery, then you have seen the impact of relationship with God.

Throughout the world, the lives of millions of addicted people have been changed dramatically by a lived belief in God. Before their recovery, they had disrupted the lives of many people; indeed, they know, with sorrow, that the effects of their addiction live on in the lives of those who were close to them. But now, because of their friendship with and trust in God, they live soberly and try to help others, especially other addicts; they are affecting the world in a positive way. Not only that, but if they follow a twelve-step program, they try to make amends for the damage they caused when they were "insane."

If religious practice and friendship with God did not have a positive effect on the larger world through changes in the attitudes and behavior of believers, we would have to say that they were empty and useless endeavors. Religion gets a bad name when its adherents make the world worse instead of better. Pious but brutal dictators, holier-than-thou types who demean those under them, devout businesspeople who gouge the poor—such people are the fodder for novels and plays that satirize unreal religion. But such Uriah-Heep types make their author's point precisely because we know many followers of true religion who are good friends and neighbors and who make a positive impact on daily life.

In the previous chapter, we noted that engaging in any friendship changes us and thus has an effect on the world in which we live. Friendship with God has an even deeper effect because it can transform our hearts at the deepest level.

This comes about through honest engagement with God and through paying attention to the movements within us to discern which of them are consonant with our friendship and which are not. Engaging in this friendship will move us toward greater maturity of heart, and that heart will propel our choices toward what is more in tune with God's dream for the world.

As John Macmurray said in those BBC lectures in the early 1930s, our emotions give purpose to our lives and move us to action. Hearts attuned by disciplined discernment to the heart of Christ will change how we act in every situation. Equally important is the authenticity of our lives; people know the real thing when they see it. They can tell when our actions spring from a changed heart and mind. This whole-person conversion is an ongoing process as we grow in our knowledge of and love for the God of all wisdom and love.

Our Liturgy Sends Us Out

We don't often think of Christian liturgy as a tool for change, but let's take a look at what actually happens in this liturgy. At the end of every eucharistic liturgy, my rector, Paul Holland, SJ, says, "The mass is not ended, for the Eucharist never ends, it is meant to be lived; so let us go forth in peace to love and serve the Lord and one another."

"But it's over," one might say. "We go on from here to the regular order of the day. What could he mean?"

Here is one of the situations in which our dualistic way of thinking is particularly harmful. We tend to separate what happens on Sunday from what happens in the rest of our week. Paul Holland wants to counter that illusion. If the liturgy has no effect on how we live our lives, then it is not liturgy. *Where liturgy is celebrated, God is present and active among the participants.* If nothing happens that affects the hearts of people as they act in daily life, then liturgy is an empty rite, and an ultimately boring one at that. It may well be that people complain about liturgy because it doesn't affect them either positively or negatively.

The Palestinian priest Elias Chacour provides a stark example of how liturgy can be empty and then come alive. In 1996, he became pastor of a congregation in the village of Ibillin, Israel. Both he and his congregation had suffered greatly in the seemingly endless conflict between Israelis and Palestinians, but the village was divided in convoluted ways. When he arrived, Father Chacour began preaching, to little avail, on the importance of ecumenical peace in the village.

In a note, one of his parishioners advised him first to try to bring about reconciliation within families in his own congregation. As he celebrated the Eucharist on Palm Sunday, he noticed how many people in the congregation were not at peace with one another and even refused peace as he blessed them with Christ's peace. At the end of the liturgy, he took the extraordinary step of marching to the doors of the church. He closed and locked them and removed the key. After returning to the front of the church, he told the people that he loved them but that their hatred and bitterness toward one another saddened him:

> This morning while I celebrated the liturgy, I found someone who is able to help you. . . . This person who can reconcile you is Jesus Christ, and he is here with us. We are gathered in his name, this man who rode in triumph into Jerusalem with hosannas ringing in his ears.
>
> So on Christ's behalf, I say this to you: The doors of the church are locked. Either you kill each other right here in your hatred and then I will celebrate your funerals gratis, or you use this opportunity to be reconciled together before I open the doors of the church. If that reconciliation happens, Christ will truly become your Lord, and I will know I am becoming your pastor and your priest. That decision is now yours.[12]

After ten minutes of what must have been a shocked and painful silence, a villager who served as an Israeli police officer stood up and asked forgiveness of everyone there and forgave everybody. Then he asked God for forgiveness and, with tears streaming down his face, embraced Father Chacour, who promptly asked everybody to embrace one another. Then "tears and laughter mingled as people who had said such ugly words to each other or who had not spoken to each other in many years now were sharing Christ's love and peace." At the conclusion, he encouraged them to go out to the whole village bringing the joy of Jesus' resurrection along with his forgiveness and reconciliation to all. He knew that this was only a beginning, but nonetheless, without this beginning, the village would have no future as a community. Liturgy, even though not the one they expected, brought this congregation face-to-face with God, and the consequences reached beyond the walls of that church building.

True liturgy, like true personal prayer, is not a spectator sport; it changes us and, as a result, has an effect on the world through our changed selves. Friendship with God, if it is real, will make a real effect, and for the better.

■ 5

Wherever Life
Places Us

*Go into all the world and proclaim the
good news.*

—MARK 16:15

What does it mean to participate in God's grace-filled work
in this world—to cooperate in the divine family business, as
it were? Is that primarily the business of people who have a
special call, a vocation, and especially those whose vocation
is work directly involved with the church?

But God's family business is the world, not the church.
The church has a special role in the family business, but
God creates the world, of which the church is only a part,
and God's dream has to do with how the entire universe
functions, not just with how the church functions. All of us
human beings are created for friendship with God and, as
adults at least, are invited to help God bring about the divine
hope for all things. No one is excluded from this invitation.

We are desired into existence to be friends of God and part of God's dream, not part of the nightmare that runs counter to God's dream. Everyone, therefore, has a calling, a vocation. And that vocation is simply to be a friend of God. As we live out that one glorious calling, we do become part of God's dream for our world, which is the kingdom of God preached by Jesus.

This is an important truth: As believers in the resurrected Jesus, we are invited to live in this world as a people who believe that, in Jesus, the new heavens and new earth are already present. What I'm talking about, and will now explore more fully, is a universal vocation.

We Bring about God's Rule through Friendship, not Coercion

When we pray the Our Father, we say, "Thy kingdom come, thy will be done on earth as it is in heaven." What is the kingdom or reign of God for which we pray? It does not refer to a place beyond this world. God creates this world to be the place where God "rules."

I put "rules" in quotation marks because it is so easy to get wrong what God's "ruling" might mean. Most often when we think of someone ruling, we imagine the ruler as controlling by power how things work. Rule means a police force of some kind, perhaps an army, and laws that are enforced, with the threat of punishment if those laws are not obeyed.

In Matthew, Mark, and Luke, temptations in the desert follow Jesus' baptism in the Jordan River by John the Baptist. We can argue that, at the baptism, the Father confirmed Jesus in his vocation to be the Messiah, the one who initiates God's final coming to rule, and that, in the desert, he confronts questions of how to be Messiah. The Tempter tells him how he can use his power:

- to feed himself miraculously: turn stones into bread
- to make a big splash that will prove who he is: throw himself off the pinnacle of the temple so that angels will miraculously rescue him, thus enthralling all who see it
- to take over the world for God by force: worship Satan, who will then turn over all power to every nation on earth

Jesus recognizes all these suggestions as temptations. Although the end results would be desirable (food, recognition as the Messiah, authority that is recognized), the means to acquire those results are not ways in which God rules.

If what we have been reflecting on up to now is true, then our petition, "Thy kingdom come, thy will be done, on earth as it is in heaven," asks that all people become friends of God, friends of one another, and friends of the universe. Such a rule cannot be coerced into existence. God cannot have the fulfillment of this dream without the willing cooperation of us human beings—because friendship cannot be coerced. So God's rule cannot come about through violence or force, but only through our acceptance of God's offer of friendship and our attempts to live out the consequences of that friendship, with the help of God's Spirit.

God's rule will come about only by our following the way of Jesus, a way he himself describes in the Sermon on the Mount in Matthew's Gospel, chapters 5–7. The sermon begins with the Beatitudes, the last of which are "Blessed are the peacemakers. . . . Blessed are those who are persecuted for righteousness' sake. . . . Blessed are you when people revile you and persecute you and utter all kinds of evil against you falsely on my account" (Matthew 5:9–11). Jesus himself lived the Beatitudes in his short public life on earth. We are asked to follow him.

Our Vocation Exists in the Here and Now

The Sermon on the Mount can be understood as proclaiming the vocation of all human beings. This vocation is compatible with any way of life or work. We don't necessarily have to change what we are now doing to become part of God's solution for our old earth. We only have to take seriously that we are daughters and sons of God, other Christs, wherever life places us.

We don't have to become monks or nuns or ministers. Just recall that Jesus was not a priest in his religion; he had no status that singled him out to act as he did. He was what all of us are, created in God's image, a human being called to live as God would live in this world.

Here's something to ponder. Notice how Jesus reacted to Zacchaeus, the chief tax collector in Jericho, mentioned in Luke 19:1–10. His fellow Jews in Jericho despised Zacchaeus because he was enriching himself at their expense and collaborating with the hated Romans. No pious Jew would have wanted to have dinner with him. But Jesus saw him in the sycamore tree and called out to him.

Usually teachers and homilists concentrate on Zacchaeus's eagerness to see Jesus as what draws Jesus' attention to him. Let's imagine a different scenario, that Zacchaeus climbed the tree out of idle curiosity and looks at Jesus with some contempt. He might be thinking, *This Jesus isn't much to look at; he doesn't have much money. What's all the fuss about?* Now hear Jesus' words and realize that Jesus looks beyond the surface of the man, sees some spark of humanity, and with humor says, "Hey, Zacchaeus, come on down; let's have dinner together." Perhaps just by going beyond the surface and touching that spark of humanity, Jesus awakens something deeply buried in Zacchaeus.

I was prompted to read the story of Zacchaeus in this way after reading the novel *Eternity, My Beloved*, by Jean Sulivan, the pen name of a priest in France. It's a story about a worker priest, Jerome Strozzi, after World War II. Strozzi had been a seminary professor, but something drew him to spend the latter part of his life in the red-light district of Paris, befriending prostitutes, pimps, and other unsavory characters. He did not try to convert them; he just spent time with them and gradually became their friend and helped them out. Many changed their lives as a result, but they did not become angels, just more alive and loving human beings. At one point in the novel, the narrator asks a question:

> "Jerome Strozzi, quote me the first phrase of the Gospel that comes to your mind."
>
> "I am the life."
>
> There's no hesitation—the answer flashes out. In dealing with the men and women he encounters every day, he has the heartbreaking sense of a humanity that is not quite human, but which desperately longs to be so. When he's about to meet someone, he has one prayer: "Through me let her find what she is looking for. Let me try to be the other, and bring to life in myself what, in spite of appearances, is true in her." Strozzi has a love for life even in its lowest manifestations. On its every level he has an intimation of *that* which transcends life's limits.[13]

Like Jesus with Zacchaeus, Strozzi looks for the often deeply hidden spark of humanity that desperately longs to come to life in the prostitutes and pimps and other broken people he encounters.

Can't we all do as much in our ordinary dealings with those we meet, try to meet them as fellow human beings who are longing to experience the peace that surpasses all understanding, the peace God dreams for all of us? You'll notice that Strozzi prayed before he went out to meet people, prayed that he might be able to let others find what they were most deeply looking for. Every day before we leave our homes, we could pray as Strozzi did. God only knows how much our world would be different if we all did that much.

Real People Are Changing the World

In the chapters to follow, you will meet ordinary people whose friendship with God has made a difference in at least a small part of the world. Some have been enabled to forgive the seemingly unforgiveable; others have been moved to compassion and found themselves and others changed as a result. In the previous chapter, we met Audrée, who had such a strong influence on Felix Frankfurter. A woman I know, a chaplain in a large city hospital, has transformed the lives of hundreds of patients and staff because she meets them with a profound sense of God's compassionate love.

She is the heart and hands of God in that hospital, yet she would say that she is doing only what comes naturally.

Try to think of an unlikely person to whom this idea of an adult friendship in the family of God could apply. Let's consider Darrell Jones, imprisoned for life for a murder he did not commit, whom I visit regularly. He could spend all his waking hours bewailing his fate and hating those who have put him in this situation. But he, too, is asked to be an adult friend of God, to discern how to act in his circumstances. Darrell had lived a hard life before his arrest for murder; he admits that he did not live on the right side of the law both before his arrest and in prison, although he never murdered anyone. But in prison, he began to care for a woman who visited and cared for him. He realized, he told me, that because he cared for her he could no longer lead the kind of life he was leading. He has become more religious, reads the Bible for inspiration and insight, and has turned his life over to God. He tries to care for his sons even though he is in prison, knowing that they are in danger of being drawn into the gang life that permeates some of the neighborhoods of Boston. Even after one of his sons was killed in gang violence, he continues to do what he can with his fellow prisoners to change things in the neighborhoods from which they come and in the prison itself. So even in the most unlikely situations we can choose to live as friends of God and part of God's solution to the problems that blight our communities.

Ask yourself how you are being called by God to be a friend, someone who brings the kingdom of God to your own small part of the universe. Let God know your own situation, your cares and concerns, and ask God to show you the part you have to play.

∷A Nightly Examination

One practice that can help you realize your part in God's dream for this world is the Examination of Consciousness developed by Ignatius of Loyola. It's a rather easy form of prayer, one that can become a habit that will build a sturdy foundation for daily life.

1. You begin by thanking God for your life and day.
2. Then you ask God to help you see your day through God's eyes, to become aware of what happened in the day that revealed you to be part of God's solution or part of the problem.
3. Then recall the various parts of the day. Notice the feelings that surface in you, both positive and negative. Ask God to help you sort out the more significant of those feelings, to make sense of them. What do they tell you about your friendship with God? For instance, you may notice how your heart was lifted when someone

spoke of her son's success. Did you tell her? If
you did, what was her reaction? If you didn't,
would it have been a good thing to do? You may
notice that you were snappish with a coworker,
and that he seemed to shrivel in front of you. In
God's presence, how do you now react to that
event? Do you feel moved to follow up on that
exchange? ::

The Jesuit writer Dennis Hamm calls this kind of daily
exercise "rummaging for God"[14] in an article reproduced at
the end of this book. He gives a fine description of how to
go about it. Doing this kind of examination of consciousness every evening will gradually attune you to how God is
touching you and moving you in ordinary life, drawing you
into friendship and into your specific part of God's loving
activity. The daily examination is a disciplined way to allow
God to transform your heart into a heart like that of Jesus.

What a privilege each of us is given just by being born:
to be invited into friendship with God and, as adults, to participate freely and joyfully with all that God is doing, every
day, right where we live. And we can take the offer and run
with it, no matter our particular path in life.

How do you react to this reflection?

6

Freedom from Fear

Do not let your hearts . . . be afraid.
—JOHN 14:27

In 1961, the musical *Carnival* gave us the popular song "Love Makes the World Go 'Round." What a hopeful thought—that love and only love fuels the world!

But so often it seems that love's opposites—hate, distrust, apathy, and vengeance—make the world go 'round. The major economies of the world would grind to a halt if love were the primary motivating force; after all, most of them depend on military spending, polluting industries, and overconsumption, with little or any thought for the future of the planet and the plight of the poor.

Although we wish that love would make the world go 'round, often enough, fear does. But it's not the fear that the Bible encourages us to nurture: a reverent acknowledgment of God as Creator and ultimate source for all. The fear that runs rampant in this world is the kind that poisons personal relationships, walls us up in gated communities, keeps us from helping our neighbors in trouble, moves us to want bigger prisons, and propels the weapons industries of the world. It leads to a society in which everyone watches his or her own back, in which everyone cares for him- or herself. Fear does seem to make our world go 'round—or at least it keeps the world churning.

In a series of Lenten talks on BBC Radio in 1964, Scottish philosopher John Macmurray made a similar diagnosis and stated that fear was the root of much of the evil in our world. In this context, he then spoke of Jesus' mission:

> So this was the mission of Jesus as I saw it. To conquer fear in the hearts of men and replace it by confidence and trust: to relieve us from life on the defensive, and replace it by a life of freedom and spontaneity: to make life rich and full in place of the thin and anxious existence to which our fears condemn us. If you doubt my interpretation, then listen to his own statement of his mission: "I am come," says the record, "I am come that they might have life and that they might have it more abundantly."[15]

To see the truth of this, we can merely reflect on a sampling of Jesus' sayings about faith:

- to the disciples frightened by the storm at sea: "Why are you afraid, you of little faith?" (Matthew 8:26)
- to the woman with a hemorrhage who touched his cloak: "Take heart, daughter; your faith has made you well." (Matthew 9:22)
- to Peter, who was about to drown after walking on the water: "You of little faith, why did you doubt?" (Matthew 14:31)
- to the disciples astounded by the destruction of the fig tree: "Whatever you ask for in prayer with faith, you will receive." (Matthew 21:22)
- to the blind Bartimaeus: "Go; your faith has made you well." (Mark 10:52)
- in a discourse to his disciples on not worrying or being afraid: "But if God so clothes the grass of the field, which is alive today and tomorrow is thrown into the oven, how much more will he clothe you—you of little faith!" (Luke 12:28)

Clearly, for Jesus, faith has to do with trust in God, and its opposite is fear. Jesus seems to be saying that the evidence of our faith is our lack of fear. In this chapter, I want to continue the theme of how friendship changes the real world by focusing on how that friendship removes our fears or, at least, diminishes them.

There Is Fear That Helps and Fear That Hurts

When Jesus urges people not to fear, he isn't referring to the normal fear response that God designed for our protection. When we smell smoke, that fear alerts us to do something. Helpful fear moves us to deal with the situation. But the fear that Jesus spoke of is the kind that immobilizes us. Hurtful fear makes it difficult, if not impossible, to deal with the situation in a helpful way. Fear of starvation will lead a man to plant food and to do whatever he can to save the crops. But if things come to the point at which he fears death for himself and his family, he may forget that he can call on his extended family or neighbors or fellow citizens for help. He may lose all hope, in which case he becomes immobilized. Such feelings lead not to positive action, but only to despair or to desperate measures that make matters worse.

During the storm at sea (Matthew 8:23–27), Peter and at least some of the other apostles in the boat were seasoned fishermen who knew how to deal with the usual storms on the Sea of Galilee. Fear must first have led them to do everything they had learned to avert peril. But as the storm worsened and it seemed that disaster and, perhaps, death were about to come upon them, they panicked and stopped doing what they could do. Lucky for them, they had Jesus in the boat. The fear Jesus opposes is the kind of fear that to some extent removes from us the freedom to act in a positive manner.

A man I know fears the anger or even disapproval of others so much that he engages in what he knows to be irrational activity so as not to meet people who might get angry at him. He avoids some of his ordinary daily activities or takes roundabout routes for fear that he will meet them. Clearly, this kind of fear is immobilizing.

The kind of fear Jesus means can occur in our friendships. With our friends we want to live in mutual trust. But fear easily gets in the way of such trust. You are my friend, and I trust you. One day, however, I hear something about you that makes me wonder about your friendship. Another friend tells me that you said that I was too touchy at times. Instead of asking you about it, because I am afraid of upsetting our friendship, I keep it to myself. However, what you said keeps bothering me, even when I am with you. I no longer feel free with you. A seed of mistrust has been introduced into our friendship.

The only way that the friendship can be righted is by my asking you about the remark and telling you how upset I was at hearing it. But I can't do that because I fear losing your friendship. Instead of caring for you and our friendship, which is what healthy friendship entails, I now begin to care for myself and don't trust you. The only way we can live as friends is by trusting each other, by my caring for you and your caring for me. If I cared for you, I would tell you about what I heard and my reactions and thus free you to care for me, if you wanted to. In this case, I would trust that you will want to, but I do not try to control your reactions to me by keeping secret what I have heard and how hurt I was. We all want to live in friendship and trust, at least with those who are close to us. But the only way that is possible is through a trust that drives out fear.

Harmful Fear Leads to Insanity

The problem, of course, is that we seem to imbibe fear with our mother's milk. Fear sits deep in our psyches and throws a spanner into even our closest relationships. This fear also bedevils relationships between neighbors, between fellow citizens of the same country, between people of different races and creeds, and between countries. It seems that Macmurray was right: fear poisons our world and leads to many of the horrors that beset us. Economic upheavals, starvation, wars, and even ecological disasters usually stem from our fear of one another.

When we are afraid, we begin to hedge our bets on God, begin to hoard like the rich man in the Gospel story who built bigger and bigger barns (Luke 12:16–21). The temptation in the garden of Genesis is based on fear. The serpent insinuates that God is a rival to be feared rather than a Father to be loved. If the man and woman eat of the tree of the knowledge of good and evil, they will be like God and will never die. When they give in to that temptation, they show their distrust in God and thus their fear. As a result, *they run away from their friendship with God*; they no longer believe in God as the good Creator. Given the reality of the good world God creates and the goodness God has already demonstrated in relationship with the man and woman, their fear is irrational. In this regard, they've gone insane—they have acted in a way inconsistent with their reality. What they tried to gain by their own efforts, they already possess by God's goodwill and grace. To make matters worse, out of their new fear of God, they try to hide, which is futile and ultimately self-defeating.

Yes, I used the word *insane*. If we are created for friendship with God and with all human beings, then the kind of fear Jesus identifies as being in opposition to faith is irrational. This fear is not only unreasonable but also against the very nature God created within us. Genesis 3 presents the fall of the first human beings as the crazy choice to become like God by disobeying God. By taking on God's role, they thought they could control their lives.

Our need to control life is related directly to our fear. An Ignatian term for this fear is *inordinate attachment*. An inordinate attachment is anything we rely on to the extent that it weakens our relationship with God and with others. Some inordinate attachments become full-blown addictions. And whenever we are that dependent on something, we develop a lifestyle of fear because we are afraid of losing that to which we are so attached.

This kind of fear leads to self-defeating and sinful behavior. We may be so attached to our investments that we live in fear that they will lose their value. We may be so attached to particular persons that we live in fear of losing them. We may be so attached to alcohol that we constantly wonder when we can get the next drink. Anything can become the focus of such fear, and fear that controls us so completely is indeed a form of insanity.

In this context, what is my definition of *insanity*? It is the belief that we cannot live without our inordinate attachments, whatever they are. In what is known as the "Big Book" of Alcoholics Anonymous, one woman describes such an insane belief:

> And still by the time I was thirty years old I was being pushed around with a compulsion to drink that was completely beyond my control. I couldn't stop drinking. I would hang on for sobriety for short intervals, but always there would come the tide of an overpowering *necessity* to drink and, as I was engulfed in it, I felt such a sense of panic that I really believed I would die if I didn't get that drink inside.[16]

Our inordinate attachments or addictions become idols. In becoming the center of our existence and the source to which we turn constantly, they take the place of God. This is insanity indeed. Of course, many of us get away with it for years because we appear to be sane. In an insane world, sanity and insanity easily pass for their opposites. (Remember, according to Mark's Gospel, Jesus' family wondered about his sanity, and the religious leaders considered him possessed by a demon [Mark 3:20–35]). But the "cure" for our fear—which the substance or activity or other person provides—is only temporary; and gradually, but almost inexorably, we need more and more of that cure to quell our fears. The rich man in the parable built bigger and bigger barns. Jealous fear of losing a loved one takes up more and more of my energies. Our insanity may become increasingly evident to others and even to ourselves. If we are fortunate, such evidence forces us to face the truth. We are offered a glimpse into our insanity and there find God patiently waiting to welcome us back to sanity.

God's Friends Choose a Sane Life

Over the past year or so, I have been impressed by the number of people who are grateful for things that seem quite frightful: depressed people grateful that they got depressed, sick people grateful for their sickness, alcoholics grateful that they are alcoholics, and even one man grateful for the recession of 2008–2009. Many of them have said something like this: "I am grateful because the depression (or alcoholism, cancer) drew me back to God. I had lost contact with God, and now I've come back home." In *The Mountain of*

Silence, Kyriacos Markides recalls this conversation with the Cypriot Abbot Maximos:

> "Remember, whatever good or bad things happen to us, they have only one single purpose, to awaken us to the reality of God and help us on the path toward union with Him. There is no other reason for being born on this planet, believe me. It is up to us whether or not we take advantage of these wake-up calls."[17]

A conversation in Gerard Goggins's novel *Anonymous Disciple* makes this point. The novel is based on the lives of two now-deceased Jesuits who found peace and serenity and even joy in the fellowship of AA. In this scene, Fred visits Jim, the talkative one and the protagonist of the novel, late one night in the hospital. Jim engages in this soliloquy:

> I wonder what kind of man I would be if I was not an alcoholic. I wonder what kind of Jesuit. I'd probably be proud and off the track. I'd have wound up being an apostate or a ladies' man. I would have been a disgrace to the Society. And instead, because I'm an alcoholic and because of AA and because of you, Fred, I have found love and peace and fulfillment. I have found friendship, and I have found my vocation even if it's not the one I expected.[18]

Jim was grateful for his alcoholism because it brought him back to friendship with God and with many other people as broken as he had been and still was. Moreover, he was a very happy man who drew people to him as light draws insects.

When I was provincial superior of my province in the 1990s, I said at one of our assemblies, and only half jokingly: "When we entered the Society of Jesus, we didn't have to believe in God; we could believe in the Church which was growing by leaps and bounds, or in the Society of Jesus, which was also enjoying the same kind of success. Now, with our numbers declining and our seminaries and novitiates half empty, we can find out whether or not we believe in God."

When things are going well for us, we can easily forget our Maker, imagining that everything is going so well because we are so good or so smart or so capable; and we can just as easily get into the mind-set of believing that we deserve all the good things we have. We may even harbor, deep in our hearts, the unspoken thought that God is quite lucky to have us on the team.

I have recently said that I am grateful that I'm an alcoholic because generally I'm so competent that I easily forget that everything I have is a gift from God. At least in this one area, I had to admit my absolute need for God. It has led me to the further realization of how much I use my competence to give me the illusion of control, thus leading me to anxiety and fear when deadlines loom or my vaunted memory begins to decline.

We might say that the act of faith in God is a three-step process, similar to the first three steps of AA:

- **The first step is to recognize that we are powerless over some aspect of our life or behavior.** This recognition is the beginning of wisdom because we are powerless over more than alcohol or whatever else we have named; ultimately, we are powerless over life itself. Some of us, maybe a great many of us, need to be brought up short before we come to this realization.

- **The second step begins with "coming to believe that a Power greater than ourselves could restore us to sanity."** In other words, we come to believe in the existence of God, a God who is waiting for our return like the father of the prodigal son in Luke 15. But the second step remains only notional if it is not followed by the third step.

- **The third step is to make "a decision to turn our will and our lives over to the care of God as we understand Him."** This step is the act of faith. I put my uncontrollable life in God's hands in trust and hope, and then I do what I can to let God do the job of saving me.

Faith requires the action of turning our lives over to God; in fact, it requires a repeated action every moment of our lives. Thus, faith is a way of life. We can live without anxious fear only insofar as we can turn our lives over to God. Sanity depends on the third step, and that dependence never ends. Hence, in a real sense, all sane people are recovering addicts, because sane people are aware of how fragile faith is and how easily they can succumb to idol worship.

But, lest we lose heart, we need to keep returning to one of the great prayers of the New Testament. In Mark's Gospel, Jesus meets a father whose son is possessed by a demon. The man says to Jesus, "But if you are able to do anything, have pity on us and help us." Jesus replies, "If you are able!—All things can be done for the one who believes." And the father blurts out, "I believe; help my unbelief!" (Mark 9:14–29) I constantly use this prayer and recommend it to others. Like this man's faith, our faith, in practice, is small. Yet small though it is, we do believe. But we need to pray continually, "Help my unbelief." That is, "Help me believe more and more fully; help me give up my futile attempts to control my life by my own efforts. Help me enjoy life, not live in terror of it."

The Holy Spirit Frees Us from Fear

What does Jesus offer us that will enable us to live without fear, or at least with our fears so lessened that we can act with trust toward others? John Macmurray noted that, besides the injunction to trust in God, Jesus also offered another one, namely to "love one another as I have loved you" (John 15:12).

How does this additional commandment help when fear keeps us from loving one another? Notice that Jesus says, "As I have loved you." It comes down to what we reflected on in chapter 2: God loves us first and unconditionally. God is love, friendship. To be freed of fear, we need to experience in faith who God is, to hear Jesus say to us what he said to his disciples at the Last Supper: "As the Father has loved me, so I have loved you; abide in my love" (John 15:9). If we experience this unconditional love in faith, then our fears are removed or at least greatly mitigated.

It's crucial for us to remember that fear is not the only resident in our hearts. Jesus promised us the Spirit, and we have received that Spirit at baptism. In John's Gospel, the resurrected Jesus appears to his fearful and cowering disciples in the upper room:

> When it was evening on that day, the first day of the week, and the doors of the house where the disciples had met were locked for fear of the Jews, Jesus came and stood among them and said, "Peace be with you." After he said this, he showed them his hands and side. Then the disciples rejoiced when they saw the Lord. Jesus said to them again, "Peace be with you. As the Father has sent

me, so I send you." When he had said this, he breathed
on them and said to them, "Receive the Holy Spirit."
(John 20:19–22)

With this scene, the Gospel writer indicates that creation is
being renewed, that the new heavens and new earth have
already begun to take over our world. Just as the breath or
spirit of God was present in the first creation in Genesis 1,
so it is now at the inauguration of the new heavens and the
new earth. When Jesus breathes the Spirit into them, the
disciples are enabled to become what they are created to
be, images of God in this world. The presence of the resurrected Jesus and the gift of the Holy Spirit remove their fear
and bring them peace. And Jesus now sends his disciples out
into the world just as his Father sent him.

In the second chapter of the Acts of the Apostles, we
find another tradition of how the Holy Spirit came upon
the disciples, but the results are similar. Here we read of a
great wind (another translation for the Greek word *pneuma*,
also translated as "breath" or "spirit") and of tongues of fire.
After this experience, Peter boldly speaks about Jesus to
the people who rushed to see what had happened. Fear no
longer imprisons him and the other disciples, as the following chapters show.

At one point, after the high priest and other elders
had questioned Peter and John and ordered them "not to
speak or teach at all in the name of Jesus" (Acts 4:18), they

answered: "Whether it is right in God's sight to listen to you rather than to God, you must judge; for we cannot keep from speaking about what we have seen and heard" (Acts 4:19–20). Then Peter and John came back to the other disciples and told them what had happened. The whole assembly praised God. "When they had prayed, the place in which they were gathered together was shaken; and they were all filled with the Holy Spirit and spoke the word of God with boldness" (Acts 4:31). Clearly, the Spirit's presence in their hearts had dispelled the kind of fear that had immobilized them after Jesus' death.

In the poem "One Heart," Franz Wright sums up the message of this chapter:

> It is late afternoon and I have just returned from
> the longer version of my walk nobody knows
> about. For the first time in nearly a month, and
> everything changed. It is the end of March, once
> more I have lived. This morning a young woman
> described what it's like shooting coke with a baby
> in your arms. The astonishing windy and altering
> > light
> and clouds and water were, at certain moments,
> You.
> There is only one heart in my body, have mercy
> on me.

The brown leaves buried all winter creatureless
        feet
running over dead grass beginning to green, the
        first scent-
less violet here and there, returned, the first star
        noticed all
at once as one stands staring into the black water.
Thank You for letting me live for a little as one of the
sane; thank You for letting me know what this is
like. Thank You for letting me look at your
        frightening
blue sky without fear, and your terrible world
        without
terror, and your loveless psychotic and hopelessly
lost
with this love.[19]

Wright is different because of his relationship with God, and, as a result, the world in which he lives and moves is different.

Love casts out fear, gives us back our sanity, and helps us look at the troubles of our world with trust, not terror. And people who trust are free to make a positive impact in any situation.

Imagine a world in which trust, and not fear, was the great energy and motivation. We would meet strangers and, without a thought, greet them with courtesy and kindness. No matter what our skin color or nationality, we could walk down any street in New York, São Paulo, Mumbai, or any other city without fear. Neighborhoods would be real communities in which people were ready to help one another in time of need. There would be no restricted neighborhoods; gated communities would be unnecessary. The social-welfare network in every country would be such that no one feared the loss of a job or an illness. Nations would care as much for the welfare of other nations as for themselves. Muslims and Jews in the Middle East, Indians and Pakistanis in Asia, Catholics and Protestants in Northern Ireland, and Hutus and Tutsis in Rwanda and Burundi would live in peace and mutual respect. The standing armies of all nations would be reduced to a minimum. The threat of nuclear destruction would no longer hang over our world. Just imagining such a world helps us realize how much fear rules our daily lives and how attractive God's dream is.

7

Forgiveness as a Way of Life

But there is forgiveness with you,
so that you may be revered.

—PSALM 130:4

Although Jesus did rise from the dead, thus inaugurating the kingdom of God here on the earth, our world is not yet under the rule of God. The wolf does not live with the lamb; swords are not beaten into ploughshares. Indeed, our world often seems to be moving in the opposite direction from what God dreams. It is awash in blood spilled because of family feuds, ethnic and religious hatred, and remembrance of wrongs done. Resentment, hatred, and the lack of forgiveness seem to rule many of the relationships between individuals and groups. In some families, a wrong done decades ago still keeps fathers and mothers, sons and daughters, and siblings apart and their families in tension. People from all walks of life want vengeance for wrongs done to them or to their loved ones. As a result, in the United States, a politician who advocates the abolition of the death penalty risks defeat at the polls. I'm sure that you can multiply examples from your own experience of how unforgiven offenses continue to warp relationships everywhere. What does friendship with God offer in this situation?

We might be tempted to say that religion offers nothing good to counteract the world's animosity. After all, many of the resentments and hatreds that poison our individual and social relationships seem to have religious origins. A Christian marries a Jew, a Muslim marries a Christian, or a Hindu marries a Muslim; the families of both parties may invoke religious reasons for declaring them anathema. In some countries and cultures, such a marriage outside the rules might lead to the killing of one or both parties, a killing that would be "justified" on religious grounds. Religion seemed to fuel the protracted violence between Protestant and Catholic Christians in Northern Ireland, although that conflict certainly had political components. In African countries where war has gone on for decades, it's difficult to tell how much of the conflict is religious and how much is ethnic or racial. Often enough, our current "wars" on terrorism are framed as conflicts between Christian and Muslim values. In *The Class of Civilizations*, Samuel P. Huntington developed the influential but disputed thesis that cultural and religious identity would be the primary source of conflict after the end of the Cold War between the United States and the Soviet Union.[20]

God Is Love That Forgives

Yet most religions affirm that God wants peace between peoples, and the majority (sometimes a silent majority) of Christians, Muslims, Jews, Hindus, Buddhists, and others seek ways to help people live together peacefully. To do so, they have to proclaim forgiveness as a primary need of the human family. A prayerful reading of the Bible reveals to us a God who *is* forgiving love. Over and over throughout history, human beings have found that God embraces them in forgiveness when they confess their sins. Psalm 130 is one example among many:

> Out of the depths I cry to you, O LORD.
>   Lord, hear my voice!
> Let your ears be attentive
>   to the voice of my supplications!
>
> If you, O LORD, should mark iniquities,
>   Lord, who could stand?
> But there is forgiveness with you,
>   so that you may be revered.

I wait for the LORD, my soul waits,
>   and in his word I hope;
my soul waits for the Lord
>   more than those who watch for the morning,
>   more than those who watch for the morning.

O Israel, hope in the LORD!
>   For with the LORD there is steadfast love,
>   and with him is great power to redeem.
It is he who will redeem Israel
>   from all its iniquities.

In the parable of the prodigal son, which might more aptly be called the prodigal (lavish) father (Luke 15:11–32), Jesus taught that sinners would experience God's forgiveness. We Christians believe that God entered our world as one of us to bring about the forgiveness of our sins. L. Gregory Jones puts it this way:

> In the incarnation Christ becomes vulnerable to the world of human beings. He becomes vulnerable not only to our capacity for created goodness and forgiveness and love and joy but also, and more determinatively, to the manifold ways in which people inevitably diminish, betray, oppress, abandon, and kill one another. But though he is vulnerable to them, he does not allow himself or us to be defined by them. Rather, Jesus' refusal

to participate in those cycles of betrayal, vengeance and violence judges all of humanity in its sin.

Christ's ministry is marked by a persistent breaking down of barriers, declaring that God's forgiveness is present for all. Indeed, Christ judges others in the righteousness of God precisely by embodying forgiveness as a way of life.[21]

The best example of this forgiving way of life occurred on Good Friday, when Jesus, dying horribly on the cross, prayed, "Father, forgive them; for they do not know what they are doing" (Luke 23:34)—and this about a crowd who was screaming and cursing at him. While this horror was perpetrated, God continued to sustain the world and did not retaliate in kind.

So the question of what it means to be a friend of God draws us toward the topic of forgiveness. If we are images of God, and if we live truly as friends of God, we are called to forgive those who have offended us. And given what we have experienced in this world—one crisscrossed by the blind alleys down which bitterness and resentment lead us—we know that the future of our world depends on a critical mass of people learning to let go of hate and embrace forgiveness.

We Are Created to Imitate Jesus

"But Jesus was sinless, and we are not," you might say. "How can we imitate him?" Sinlessness does not mean that Jesus did not suffer temptation. To be human is to become part and parcel of human magnanimity and compassion as well as human betrayal, violence, and sin. Perhaps Paul was referring to this aspect of what it means for God to become human when he said, "For our sake he [God] made him [Jesus] to be sin who knew no sin, so that in him we might become the righteousness of God" (2 Corinthians 5:21). L. Gregory Jones writes: "Jesus' sinlessness consists in his ability to suffer human evil, particularly the human tendency toward destructive judgment, and to absorb it without passing it on."[22]

In other words, for Jesus, forgiveness was a way of life. Jesus was a human being intimately involved with this world of human folly and sin, but he refused to be mastered by it, thus showing us that it is possible to live as an image of God in a world that holds so much violence and sorrow. Jesus lived a human life as God's true son, overcoming the temptations all of us are heir to by being born into this world. Thus he demonstrated that it is possible to lead such a way of life. But to do so we must believe in God in an effective way, in a way that banishes or at least reduces our fears enough so that we can try to live as Jesus did.

Jesus' way of life was, as we know, not without cost; it cost him his life, and it has cost the lives of countless others down the centuries since Jesus' time. The kingdom of God that Jesus not only preached but also embodied is a kingdom of peace and communion among all people. This kingdom is a threat to all kingdoms that rely on power and violence to enforce their rule. Such kingdoms depend on fear and distrust of others for their hegemony. As a result, Jesus ran afoul of the leaders of his own religion and of the Roman occupiers of his country. On Good Friday, those leaders showed who had the power, but Jesus went to his death trusting that his dear Father, his Abba, would bring victory out of what seemed the total defeat of his mission.

Throughout his public life, Jesus had contrasted faith with fear. In the garden the night before his death, he seems to have faced for the last time the temptation to fear, but he was able to hand over his life in trust to his dear Father. He went to his death believing that his way of being Messiah was the way to bring about God's kingdom, and that way meant eschewing all violence and coercive power. As Jones writes, he absorbed human evil without passing it on. His faith in God made this possible. He was able to forgive even those who tortured him so cruelly.

Forgiveness Is Difficult but Necessary

Forgiveness is one of the most difficult aspects of God for us to emulate. It runs counter to our desire for vengeance, our sense of justice, of the rightness of things. Yet in the Our Father, we say, "Forgive us our trespasses as we forgive those who have trespassed against us." When I am aware of how unforgiving I often am, I shudder to think that my forgiveness of others will measure God's forgiveness of me.

In the preface to *Exclusion and Embrace*, Miroslav Volf tells the reader about his reaction when, at the end of a talk on forgiveness, the noted theologian Jürgen Moltmann asked him, "But can you embrace a *četnik*?" The *četniks* were notorious Serbian fighters who had been ravaging Volf's native Croatia with ferocious cruelty. Moltmann's question cut to the heart of Volf's talk and called his conclusion into question. Volf writes:

> I had just argued that we ought to embrace our ene-
> mies as God has embraced us in Christ. Can I embrace
> a *četnik*—the ultimate other, so to speak, the evil other?
> What would justify the embrace? Where would I draw
> the strength for it? What would it do to my identity as
> a human being and as a Croat? It took me a while to
> answer, though I immediately knew what I wanted to
> say. "No, I cannot—but as a follower of Christ I think I
> should be able to." In a sense this book is the product of
> the struggle between the truth of my argument and the
> force of Moltmann's objection.[23]

Volf's book is a dense and penetrating study that demonstrates both the difficulty and the necessity of forgiveness
and reconciliation. Our world has no future without forgiveness, as Desmond Tutu has written.[24]

Miroslav Volf clearly shows that such forgiveness and
reconciliation, the embrace of the "absolute other," can

become a reality only by God's grace. In *Free of Charge: Giving and Forgiving in a Culture Stripped of Grace*, Volf argues effectively for the need of forgiveness for the sake of our world. We may think that we can forgo revenge, and yet require retributive justice, a justice that demands measure for measure, or a punishment that befits the offense. He believes that the demand for retributive justice in a world shot through with injustice would wreak havoc; no one could claim complete innocence and thus avoid retribution. Retributive justice would force all of us to live in fear of retribution because all of us "have sinned and fall short of the glory of God" (Romans 3:23). He maintains that retributive justice cannot come about without the use of some violence. He continues:

> Revenge multiplies evil. Retributive justice contains evil—and threatens the world with destruction. Forgiveness overcomes evil with good. Forgiveness mirrors the generosity of God whose ultimate goal is neither to satisfy injured pride nor to justly apportion reward and punishment, but to free sinful humanity from evil and thereby reestablish communion with us. This is the gospel in its stark simplicity—as radically countercultural and at the same time as beautifully human as anything one can imagine.[25]

In the rest of this chapter, I want to show a way forward for us as individuals to become forgiving people. In the next chapter, I speak of ways that groups may come to forgiveness and reconciliation.

We Can Move into True Forgiveness

Stephen Yavorsky, SJ, provides an example of the difficulty of forgiveness and a way to move toward it. A trained spiritual director, Yavorsky volunteered to go to Rwanda after the genocidal killings of 1994. The Jesuit retreat center there had lost three Jesuits in the genocide and needed help to recoup. During his time at the center, where he also acted as the treasurer, Yavorsky was cheated of rather large sums of money that belonged to the center—by people whom he considered friends. He reveals how violently angry he became toward these people, even to the point of wanting them to suffer and to die for what they had done.

One day he sat down to pray, and in his imagination, he found himself hanging beside Jesus at the crucifixion. As he looked out at the crowd angrily cursing Jesus and wanting him dead, he saw among them the people he wanted dead. As Jesus began to say, "Father, forgive . . . ," Yavorsky writes, "I cut him off." He told Jesus that it was useless to forgive these people who wanted him to die in despair. At that moment, he found himself in the crowd, "having hurt him by not wanting to forgive. He was loving me along with them, and longing that at least some of us join him on the cross of forgiveness." Then he was back on the cross beside Jesus. He continues:

> I tried to look down with him at the betrayers below, but my neck would not turn. I had to do it, Jesus wanted me to, but I could not. I was drawn to look at his face. He knew them completely and loved them. At that moment I came to realize that all I had been told about our never being tempted beyond our strength was simply not true. I no longer believe it. We are very much tempted beyond our strength. I was realizing that the kind of forgiveness being asked of me was beyond my ability to grant, and beyond anyone's ability. We are not capable of it; yet it is asked of us. I saw Jesus doing it and very much wanted to be a part of him. Forgiveness was not beyond his strength.
>
> Keeping my attention entirely on him, I found myself saying, "You look at them; I'll look at you." I could at least bear to behold him forgiving them. A hard knot started to untie in me, and I felt a grudging attraction for a desire to forgive. I knew I was being fed in a different way, and that I would need to keep doing this for a long time.[26]

In this wrenching text, Yavorsky reveals much about the difficulty of forgiving and how he began to move toward being able to forgive. Let me outline some of the steps we can take when we find ourselves in situations similar to those of Volf and Yavorsky.

Step 1: Experience God's forgiving love.

One thing seems clear from both Volf's and Yavorsky's experiences: moral exhortation to be a forgiving people has limited effectiveness. Both of these men knew what they should do as Christians, but neither could do what he knew he should do. I believe that the first step toward becoming a forgiving person is to experience the love and forgiveness of God and/or of some other person. All of us who have anything to do with the formation of Christians need to keep this truth in mind: before we teach doctrine or morality, we must help people experience God's love and mercy. This is one of the reasons I insisted in chapter 2 that God loves us first and loves us unconditionally. It is hard enough for Christians like Volf and Yavorsky, who have experienced this unconditional love of God, to forgive; it would be next to impossible to do so without that experience. Also, this experience of God's unconditional love must include the experience of knowing that God's love embraces us precisely as sinners, as people who have betrayed and offended God and God's image within us. Only if we have experienced ourselves as created out of love and forgiven out of love will we be able to move toward forgiving others.

But, as Jesus makes clear in the parable of the man who was forgiven a huge debt and then jailed a man who owed him a pittance (Matthew 18:23–35), we have to receive the gift of forgiveness, which includes receiving the judgment that we have sinned. The unforgiving debtor in the parable could not have received the forgiveness of his great debt as an undeserved gift and then gone out to do what he did to his fellow worker who owed him so small a debt. We must receive God's forgiveness as what it is, an undeserved gift given to someone who has offended God deeply. If that happens, there is a possibility that we will, at least, want to forgive others.

Step 2: Acknowledge how difficult, even impossible, forgiveness is.

Both Volf and Yavorksy indicate that the next step, at least under the extreme circumstances they faced, was to acknowledge that they could not forgive. They admitted their inability to do what they wanted to do. In effect, they took the first step of AA, which is to admit one's powerlessness to do what one wants to do. For an alcoholic, that means admitting one's powerlessness to stop drinking. Yavorsky writes that he was tempted beyond his strength, Volf that he could not forgive a *četnik* even though he knew that he should be able to do so.

I have come to believe that many of us make moral demands on ourselves that lead nowhere except to despair, when the most honest thing would be to admit that we cannot do what we believe we should do. In fact, for some addicts, keeping the issue on the moral plane guarantees that they will never give up their addiction. Moral demands can actually enable continued addictive behavior. As long as I continue to ask for forgiveness for drinking too much or for not forgiving—without acknowledging my powerlessness to do either—I continue to believe that I should be able to do what I cannot do, when what I need to do is face the fact that I cannot stop drinking or let go of a grudge. And as long as I continue to try through willpower to do the impossible, I will continue to drink or to hold on to my resentment.

Step 3: Ask for God's help.

But admitting our inability or powerlessness to forgive would lead only to despair if that were the end of the story. There is the second step: "to believe that a Power greater than ourselves could restore us to sanity." God can save us from our powerlessness to forgive or to become sober or to live a chaste life or, for that matter, to live a Christian life. This second step, however, remains a mere idea unless the third one follows it, to make "a decision to turn our will and our lives over to the care of God as we understand Him." Often enough, people who admit to themselves and to God that they are powerless to do what they know they should do experience themselves as wrapped in the loving and forgiving arms of God, who loves them in their broken and impotent state.

Such an experience is a powerful antidote to the feeling of helplessness, because at least part of the feeling is rooted in the belief that we should be able to stop drinking or to forgive or to live chastely to be loved. But none of this is possible unless we ask for God's help—and ask because we know that we cannot accomplish anything without that help.

Keep in mind that, initially, Stephen Yavorsky did not want to be healed of his unforgiving heart. He did not even want Jesus to forgive the people who had injured him and others. How do we move from being unwilling to forgive to admitting our powerlessness and asking for help? Notice that Yavorsky did not run away from the terrible encounter with Jesus that resulted from his angry outburst. He could have stopped praying when he yelled at Jesus to stop or when he found himself among the jeering crowd. Something held him there. It was probably his love for Jesus; he did not want to lose Jesus. So he stayed in that awful encounter.

Often what moves us from not wanting to forgive is some realization that we are, in the process, moving away from something or someone we love. It seems that Volf and Yavorsky realized that they were moving away from Jesus—not that Jesus was abandoning them but that they were moving away from him. They found that they could not stay close to Jesus and remain unwilling to forgive. Again, notice that it was not the moral imperative to forgive but the relationship with a loving friend that did the trick. Our friendship with God moves us toward the desire to ask for a forgiving heart. We want to stay close to God, and we find that we cannot stand being close to divine love unless we are willing to ask for a forgiving heart.

For a long time, nagging questions about my consumption of alcohol had bothered me, but I never did anything about the questions except give myself rationalizing answers. One summer, almost ten years ago, I was on retreat with other members of my province. For most of the retreat, there was no alcohol available; this did not seem to bother me. However, on a feast day, we were invited to have a social gathering and dinner with the Jesuit community at the institution where the retreat took place. There alcohol was available, and I proceeded to consume my usual amount, and some more. After dinner, I sat down to pray and promptly fell asleep for a couple of hours. The retreat director had just told us this story: A man died and met Jesus. He said to Jesus, "I wish I had known you better." Jesus replied, "I wish I had known you better." The next day it hit home that I was the man in the story. Jesus did not know me as well as he wanted to because of my drinking. Now I had a very good reason to want to stop drinking alcohol. In addition, I had phoned one of my best friends the night before and slurred some words. The next day she called and told me that she could not bear hearing from me that way anymore. Now I had another reason to want to stop drinking alcohol. Love for Jesus and for my friend led me to the point at which I had to face reality, admit my powerlessness, and ask for help, which God gave me quite generously. I believe the same process works for forgiveness when we find ourselves unable and unwilling to forgive.

Grace Is Never Cheap

What these examples show, I hope, is that being a Christian is not for the faint of heart or for those who want only comfort. Becoming a friend of Jesus calls us to more and more radical honesty with ourselves and with Jesus. And what will get in the way of that friendship is not our sin or our failure to be the kind of people we want to be but our unwillingness to appear before God as we are. Often we want to come to God in our best clothes, as it were, but to do so, we have to deny a lot of the truth about ourselves. The truth is that our clothes are dirty all the time; we are not pure in any facet of our lives. We are lustful, violent at least in our thoughts and emotions, unforgiving, resentful, addicted, petty, and envious.

Yavorsky, feeling that he should be a better person and a better Christian before talking to Jesus, could have abandoned prayer until his vengeful and hate-filled thoughts and emotions were once again under control. But then he would not have been healed. He was willing to let Jesus see how vengeful he was; only in that way could he begin to let his heart be thawed. What he needed—what all of us need—is to know that God takes us as we are and wants to work with us to help us move forward with our lives.

God wants our friendship, not our perfection. If friendship with God depended on our being perfect first, we would never get out of the starting gate. What frees the heart, mind, and spirit for forward movement in any friendship, but especially in the friendship with God, is the experience of being known and loved just as we are. And that, of course, is what it means to realize that God loves us first and unconditionally.

I suspect that this is the deepest teaching of the psalms, especially those psalms that express some really terrible truths about the psalmist, for example, his near despair at God's absence (Psalm 13) or his desire for vengeance (Psalm 137). The deepest teaching is that God relates to us as we really are and works with that material.

Try this exercise: Imagine a father whose son has been shot to death telling God that he wants the murderer's own son to be killed; now imagine him feeling God's presence. As you imagine it, what do you experience? As I imagine the scene, I sense God embracing the man. The man can hardly believe it, and as he lets the experience continue, he feels his heart thawing. "If God can love me as I desire the death of another man's son, then he must also love my enemy. What that man did to my son is awful, but God still loves him as God loves me even though I myself want to do something horrible." Something has to give under such circumstances, and from experience, what gives is the unforgiving heart.

God is interested not in meeting a person I pretend to be but in meeting the real me. And it is the encounter of the real me with God that transforms my reality into something more closely resembling the image of God I am created to be.

An encounter with God does not leave us unchanged; we do not come out of it unscathed. God is the Holy One who will not allow us to remain less than who we are created to be. In Leviticus 19:2, Moses is told to tell the Israelites: "You shall be holy, for I the LORD your God am holy." We are created in God's image and likeness; hence, holiness is our destiny. We become holy, however, not by willing it but only by a sort of holy osmosis, by engaging in a personal relationship with God that transforms us, sometimes without even noticing how changed we are. We cannot do it without God's abiding friendship, grace, and help.

A man I know—let's call him Frank—told me this story. He was very angry with Joe, another member of his religious community. In prayer, he told Jesus that he had wanted to knock Joe down during a recent encounter. Jesus, with a stern gesture, said, "Are you my best friend?" "Of course." "Well," responded Jesus, "Joe is my best friend." If Frank had not told Jesus the truth, nothing would have changed in his attitude. This exchange brought home to Frank that he needed to ask Jesus for help to see Joe as Jesus saw Joe. Isn't this true for anyone we dislike or who has offended us? Everyone in this world is the apple of God's eye, God's best friend, in a way. But the only way we will come to change our attitudes toward some of these friends of God is to tell God how we feel, even though we may wish that we did not feel this way.

In recent years, psychologists and psychotherapists have learned that forgiveness has healing and restorative powers for those who forgive, not just for those who are forgiven. Robert Weber summarizes some of the research on this theme in an article in *Group Circle: The Newsletter of the American Group Psychotherapy Association*. He cites the words of George Vaillant, who analyzed data from a longitudinal study of Harvard graduates: "In short, the study participants who have aged most successfully are those who worry less about cholesterol and waistlines and more about gratitude and forgiveness."[27]

I need to say, however, that I hope such good news is only a further incentive, not the main motive, for becoming a forgiving person. That motive, I hope, will be our desire to be like our friend Jesus.

Forgiveness and Judgment Work Together

At a talk on friendship with God, someone raised the question of the final judgment. This notion of friendship with God seems to pass over in silence Jesus' own teaching. In Matthew 25:41, there are not only sheep but also goats, and the goats are told, "You that are accursed, depart from me into the eternal fire prepared for the devil and his angels." Apparently God is not all-forgiving. Why, then, should we forgive everyone, especially those who do not repent their offenses against us? The questioner did not say all of this, but I was aware of these implications in the question. What I said then is the best I have been able to arrive at through prayer and with the help of books by Miroslav Volf and others.[28]

Forgiveness of another, even forgiveness of us by God, involves judgment. If I forgive you for some injury you have done me, I am also indicating that you have injured me. If that judgment is not part of forgiveness, then there is nothing to forgive. The same is true in our relationship with God. In the presence of God, we become aware of what we have actually done that deserves condemnation and, at the same time, realize that God does not hold it against us—God, has, indeed, already forgiven it. God cannot lie; God's forgiveness, therefore, includes the judgment that we have sinned and that we fall short of the glory of God (Romans 3:23). In God's presence, we become aware of how true those words are, and yet we find that we are not condemned; we are forgiven and loved as though we had not done these things. But we did them; that cannot be avoided in God's presence because God is truth; hence, we are judged. But in this case the judgment is one of mercy, a mercy we have only to accept.

Jews and Christians believe that God will, finally, put all things in this world to rights. This is what both religions mean by believing in a just God who is creator of the universe. That final putting to rights will be a judgment, but it will be a judgment of mercy for everyone who is willing to accept the truth and the mercy. The only way, as far as I can tell, that anyone will end up outside God's new heavens and new earth is by refusing finally both the truth and the mercy, that is, the forgiving love of God. Ultimately, I believe, such a person would have to refuse to accept the reality that God is love. God does not change into a vengeful and violent God because of what we do. God's forgiving love changes us; those who refuse to change condemn themselves.

Let me also point out that our attitude toward unforgiving people may be crucial in the move toward their becoming forgiving. Often enough, when people who want vengeance—for example, those who rejoice in the execution of a criminal—are described in newspaper articles or when we see them on television, there is a not so subtle subtext in the reporting; namely, these people are worthy of contempt. We Christians need to take stock of our own reactions to such descriptions or pictures. Do I feel superior to such people? Do I want to argue with them, to tell them that their attitudes are unchristian? If I do note these feelings, then I need to ask God to help me embrace such people as God does. Perhaps then I will realize that my "enlightened" attitude may be only skin-deep because I have not been challenged by losses as others have and as Miroslav Volf and Stephen Yavorksy were. I can help unforgiving people only if I can embrace them.

Indeed, as Volf makes clear in *Exclusion and Embrace*, only by embracing the other can I really understand him or her. Again, we return to the issue of who God is and how God wants us to be with one another. Christians who cannot lovingly embrace the unforgiving are in as much need of God's forgiving love as those they cannot embrace. The unforgiving have become for them a stumbling block. Each of us desperately needs to allow God to embrace us sinners so that we will be able to embrace others and do the only kind of ministry that is truly Christian.

L. Gregory Jones sums up the argument of his book *Embodying Forgiveness* this way: "From the Christian perspective I have been developing, forgiveness is not primarily a word that is spoken or an action that is performed or a feeling that is felt. It is a way of life appropriate to friendship with the Triune God."[29]

And it is a way of life that makes an unmistakable impact on the people with whom we live and on the cultures and the nations in which we live.

8

Reconciliation on a Larger Scale

Nation shall not lift up sword against nation.
—Isaiah 2:4

In the previous chapter, we reflected on the necessity and difficulty of forgiveness between individuals. But many of the most intractable problems in the world involve resentments between and within groups. As with individuals, many group conflicts have religious roots. In addition, many Christians recognize that the divisions between their churches are a scandal, yet the pace toward reconciliation is glacial. In the Roman Catholic Church itself, the rancorous divisions about the implementation of the Second Vatican Council, about the social and moral teaching of the church, about liturgical practice, and so on, are no less scandalous.

Does a spirituality of friendship with God have anything to offer these situations? Are there instances in which such a spirituality seems to have moved people toward reconciliation, in which human beings as a group behaved as true sons and daughters of God?

It Happened in South Africa

Some of the most moving examples of people acting like God's adult children come from Archbishop Desmond Tutu's book about the Truth and Reconciliation Commission in South Africa. Aptly, he titles the book *No Future without Forgiveness*. After the end of apartheid, the instrument of national healing was the Truth and Reconciliation Commission. Forgiveness and reconciliation did not require that people deny the truth that something awful had happened; indeed, they required that the truth be told. Tutu's examples of uncommon forgiveness include white and black South Africans, although, not surprisingly, the majority of the examples come from blacks, who suffered the most from the evils of apartheid.

One example was especially touching. The Truth and Reconciliation Commission held a hearing on the massacre in the small town of Bisho. The massacre occurred in September 1992, when white commanders ordered South African soldiers, many of them black, to fire on unarmed peaceful marchers, resulting in the deaths of thirty people. As the hearing opened in Bisho, the attendees, many of whom were related to or knew those killed, were quite hostile and made even more hostile by the testimony of a major general of the army who apparently justified the shootings. Then Colonel Horst Schobesberger, one of the officers who gave the orders to shoot, spoke:

> I say we are sorry. I say the burden of the Bisho massacre will be on our shoulders for the rest of our lives. We cannot wish it away. It happened. But please, I ask specifically the victims, not to forget, I cannot ask this, but to forgive us, to get the soldiers back into the community, to accept them fully, to try to understand also the pressure they were under then. This is all I can do. I'm sorry, this I can say, I'm sorry.[30]

Tutu writes: "That crowd, which had been close to lynching them, did something quite unexpected. It broke out into thunderous applause! Unbelievable! The mood change was startling." He then spoke to the crowd, asking them to observe a moment's silence and continued: "It isn't easy, as we all know, to ask for forgiveness and it's also not easy to forgive, but we are people who know that when someone cannot be forgiven there is no future." The spirit of God was powerfully active in that room, and ordinary people allowed their hearts to be touched to ask for forgiveness and to give it.

Forgiveness is possible, even in the dire circumstances of brutal evil that one party perpetrates on another, because we are made in the image and likeness of God. God forgives us for crucifying Jesus. And, as Archbishop Tutu reminds us, our future and the future of our world, and of God's loving enterprise in the world, depend on our being able to ask for and to give forgiveness. In an article by Alex Perry about the musical *Truth in Translation*, the director, Michael Lessac, says that he aimed to tell the story of an "evolutionary step for humanity" when South Africa did "something that no other country in the world has ever done: forgive the past to survive the future." In the same article, Nelson Mandela talks about the African term *ubuntu*, referring to the fact that everyone, no matter their color, religion, or even their status as friend or enemy, is tied to everyone else. "The question is," says Mandela, "are you going to . . . enable the community around you to be able to improve?" Forgiveness is about enabling our communities to improve.[31]

Archbishop Tutu's book contains many wise counsels on how to move toward reconciliation in a very dark and dangerous time of transition for a nation. It is a remarkable testimony to the power of Christian principles in action in a concrete political situation fraught with peril for everyone. The method has been tried in other places with various degrees of success. The fall 2008 issue of *Human Development* contains two articles that detail how difficult such reconciliation can be after years of terrible violence. Matt Garr, SJ, writes about his experience on a truth and reconciliation commission in Peru and of the difficulty of such reconciliation after years of revolutionary war that included atrocities on both sides. John Katunga Murhula demonstrates the complexities of achieving reconciliation in Democratic Republic of the Congo, where so many of the problems stem from a history of exploitation by outside agencies.[32]

Groups Can Forgive One Another

Reflection on the work of South Africa's Truth and Reconciliation Commission reminded me of some group work I had done years ago on communal discernment—that is, discernment done not by individuals but by and within a group of people. This work rested on the belief that God has a stake in our communities and organizations because all of us, as sons and daughters of our triune God, are called to live in harmony and friendship with one another, whatever our groups or affiliations.

In communal discernment, a group that faces some important decision or has reached an impasse in its communal life or work comes together to seek God's help to move forward. My colleagues and I discovered that a group needed to deal with some presuppositions before group members could engage honestly in communal discernment. If they were able to meet these requirements, then the process could lead to fruitful and reconciling decisions. What are these presuppositions?

Recognize the impasse.

First, the members of the group or community have to recognize that they are at an impasse and that all of them are in this together. Unless they want to break up as a group, they have to do something together to move beyond where they now are.

Sometimes geography makes it impossible to separate. For example, in the conflict between Protestants and Catholics in Northern Ireland, as Raymond Helmick writes, the "hard men," those imprisoned from both sides for murders, came to the realization that "there was no livable future for any of their communities unless they learned to accommodate each other."[33]

Many of the conflicts in our world are of this kind: geography keeps people in contact with one another, and the only way forward is for all parties to come to a similar conclusion. Sometimes geography is also abetted by religious affiliation, for example, when Christians who are at odds reside in the same parish or belong to the same congregation. However the group has been constituted, if group members want to resolve their conflict, everyone in the group or groups needs to realize that they are in the predicament together and thus need to work it out together.

End the blame.

Second, the blaming has to end. One thing that hinders progress toward forgiveness and reconciliation is the prevalence of the blame game, in which each party in a dispute blames the other party, and neither recognizes its own contribution to the difficulty. St. Paul articulates one of the tenets of Christianity: "For there is no distinction, since all have sinned and fall short of the glory of God" (Romans 3:22–23). In any impasse within or between groups, we can say the same; of course, some are more at fault than others, but it would be rare indeed to find that one or some in a group were totally without fault. So it is important for all to recognize that the problem is "ours," not "theirs." Only in this way can we also come to the hope that we can all become part of the solution.

Develop trust.

Third, trust must be developed between those at odds, at least enough trust to begin to look seriously at how God can get this group or community out of the impasse. In part, that trust requires that enough people believe their opponents to be seeking God's help. In other words, enough of "my group" needs to trust that enough of "the others" are serious about wanting to ask God for help to a solution even if each party has to lose something in the process.

When we realized our need to work on these presuppositions with groups, we fell upon a process that is analogous to what individuals must go through to engage truthfully in the discernment of spirits. To engage in such discernment, I need to have a real trust in God based on the experience of God's everlasting love and God's forgiveness of my sins. Only when I have experienced both God's love and God's forgiveness am I in a position in which I trust God enough to seek honestly and without preconditions God's dream for me.

In a group hoping to find a resolution to the conflicts or resentments that make their communal life difficult or even impossible, such trust in God must be present in the individuals. But in addition, the individuals in the group must trust that the other members of the group have the same dispositions and sincerely want to find God's desire for the group. Reconciliation is impossible unless the members can come to a real trust in one another as sincerely wanting to find God's dream for the group.

Work through the Process

What follows is a description of some of the processes we used to help people in groups overcome their fears and entrust themselves more to one another. I have freely borrowed from chapter 11 of *Letting God Come Close*.[34]

Facilitators function somewhat as spiritual directors.

First, the facilitators explain their role as facilitators by an analogy to the role of a spiritual director. Spiritual directors do not manufacture desires or prayer experiences for those they direct but help them notice what is happening in the relationship with God, to discern what leads toward God and what leads away from God, and to decide what to do about the discernment. So the facilitators of the group try to help the group articulate what it wants from God and to help the members approach God in prayer with that desire.

Group members articulate a desire and ask God to accomplish it.

It is important to remind the individuals that they are asking God to relate to them precisely as members of this group with the group's desire, that is, to know that God has hopes for them as a group. Just as individuals ask God for what they desire, trusting that God has their good at heart, so too the individuals in a group context approach God with the group's desire, trusting that God has the good of this group at heart.

Group members acknowledge that trust must grow within the group as well as toward God.

The facilitators point out that the process is a slow one of growing in trust in God's hope for the group and in one another. Group members already trust God, but they probably have not thought much about God's desires and hopes for the group as such. And most groups need to develop a trust in one another as prayerfully and honestly searching for God's hopes for the group. Communal reconciliation and/or discernment require that each member of the group trust that God will reveal God's hopes for the group through individual prayer and through sharing the experience of that prayer. To engage in this process, I must trust that all the others are sincerely praying and trying to remain open to discerning God's will. After all, my future life in this group is on the line.

Facilitators provide a general structure for prayer.

The facilitators suggest a way for the members to approach God in personal prayer with the desire that God communicate to each one precisely as a member of the group.

- Each member prays for a period of time and then takes a few minutes for reflection.
- After the prayer period is over, members return to the group. If the group is fewer than ten to twelve people, all the sharing sessions are in one group. If it is larger, break it up into groups of ten or fewer for the sharing and ask that someone summarize for the whole group in a report.
- The facilitators help members report to one another as much as they wish of what happened during the prayer. Each session can last at least a couple of hours.
- The facilitators ask the group to try to listen without judgment to the experiences shared. Indeed, because the assumption of such group sharing is that we are hoping to hear what God is saying

to us as a group, these periods of sharing are approached, as much as possible, with the same attentive and contemplative attitude one hopes to have in private prayer.

- What happens in the sharing then gives the facilitators and the group something to work on for the next session.

Some Sample Sessions

The facilitators might suggest that in the first session they use a text like Isaiah 43:1–5 for their prayer:

> Do not fear, for I have redeemed you;
> I have called you by name, you are mine.
> When you pass through the waters, I will be with
> you;
> and through the rivers, they shall not
> overwhelm you;
> when you walk through fire you shall not be
> burned,
> and the flame shall not consume you.
> For I am the LORD your God,
> the Holy One of Israel, your Savior. . . .
>
> Because you are precious in my sight,
> and honored, and I love you,

I give people in return for you,
>   nations in exchange for your life.
Do not fear, for I am with you.

The Israelites heard these consoling words when they were in exile, their temple destroyed and their hopes at their lowest. It is more than likely that they were a community deeply divided, some blaming their leaders for their plight, others doubting God's fidelity, and still others opting to assimilate to their Babylonian captors. The facilitators suggest that the members ask God to help them hear the words of Isaiah as applying to them as members of this group.

Group members then pray privately for a period of time and afterward return to the group. Each person is then asked to share whatever he or she wishes of what happened during the prayer. Such an icebreaker can be reassuring, and the variety of experiences enlightening. In a felt way, the participants may begin to realize how sincere and faith filled each one is. They are often surprised at how easy and enjoyable it is to talk about prayer with one another. Depending on how this first session goes, the facilitators might either suggest a repetition for the next session or suggest that they ask God to help them know God's hope for them as a group.

If they do move on to the latter point, they can suggest private prayer in which each one asks God to reveal God's dream for them as a group. They might add to the text just cited the words that follow a bit later in Isaiah 43:18–21:

> Do not remember the former things,
> > or consider the things of old.
> I am about to do a new thing;
> > now it springs forth, do you not perceive it?
> I will make a way in the wilderness
> > and rivers in the desert.
> The wild animals will honor me,
> > the jackals and the ostriches;
> for I give water in the wilderness,
> > rivers in the desert,
> to give drink to my chosen people,
> > the people whom I have formed for myself
> so that they might declare my praise.

During the group meetings, facilitators remind participants to listen to one another contemplatively and to note their inner reactions as they listen and take time after the session to reflect on their reactions. God, the facilitators suggest, is present as we speak and listen to one another. If group members feel antipathy to what one member is saying, for example, they might want to ask for God's help to see things from that person's perspective.

After the group has articulated its sense of God's vision and dream for them as a group, group members might be ready to ask for God's help to discover what blocks them from realizing the dream. Now the hard part begins, because they will be addressing issues that will bring to light resentments, mistrust, and other negative emotions. For example, they might face their feelings that the others are to blame for the problems in the group or that some people will manipulate the process to get their own way, or that they are not serious about reconciliation.

Overcome Mistrust and Anger

We have been talking about groups that begin the process with some goodwill toward one another. Often enough, however, groups do not begin with much goodwill and trust. This is the case in many of the conflicts among religious groups. Then the negative feelings may have to be addressed even earlier.

One group of male members of a religious congregation displayed so much anger, resentment, suspicion, and misunderstanding at the very first session that I wondered whether we had opened Pandora's box. I had no time to confer with my colleague as to what to do. I thought of the scene of the apostles in the upper room before the appearance of the risen Jesus (John 20:19–23). With some fear and trembling, I pointed out that the community's reality had surfaced rather quickly and then suggested that members might feel as the apostles did after the Crucifixion when they boarded themselves up in the upper room. I asked them to imagine the feelings of guilt, anger, suspicion, and fear in that upper room. Into the disciples' midst came Jesus saying, "Peace be with you." I suggested that they might want to spend an hour in prayer asking Jesus to be present with the group.

When participants returned to the group the next day, the atmosphere had noticeably shifted. Where before accusations and angry denunciations of others prevailed, now each one spoke of his own fears and failings and at the same time voiced a trust that God would be with them. They had not yet reached the promised land, but they were on the way to becoming a group that eventually might be able to move forward together.

Another group of male religious who were delegates charged with the election of a new provincial had asked two of us to facilitate a four-and-a-half-day process that would help them be more discerning and open during the election that would follow. The congregation was reeling from a heavy financial blow and from departures that had left the members demoralized, angry, and suspicious. Among the group were some whom the others held responsible for their problems, especially their financial problems. Early in our sessions, feelings of anger, suspicion, guilt, and helplessness emerged. The first two days were stormy, but we could sense a gradual growth in trust. As one man said, "We have thought the unthinkable and said the unsayable."

Toward the end of the second day, we summarized the situation in this fashion:

You sense yourselves as broken, needy, helpless and sinful precisely as members of this congregation and as delegates. A number of you have identified with Simon the Pharisee who scorned Jesus for letting the sinful woman wash his feet. Some of you have expressed resentment at being put into the position of picking up the pieces of a mess caused by others. Some have expressed fears that as a group you will not have the courage to make the necessary decisions. Some of you fear that even God cannot change you. And yet you have also desired healing, have desired that Jesus make you brothers again. We suggest that you present yourselves to Jesus as you are and ask him for what you want. You might want to contemplate Jesus in the house of Simon (Luke 7:36–50) or the washing of the feet (John 13:1–16).

We also suggested speaking to Jesus on the cross and asking him to help them as a group.

The sharing after this period of prayer was very emotional and honest. One man asked with tears for the forgiveness of the group. Another reported emptiness in prayer and asked the group to pray for him. A couple of men said that the desire for healing was growing in them. Most of the others reported consolation and a sense of being healed. Tears were shed. At the end of the sharing, they broke up into groups of two or three to seek forgiveness and reconciliation. The next day, men continued to ask one another for forgiveness and reconciliation. We spent the last two days focusing on Jesus' relationship with his apostles in the Gospel of Mark. At the end of the process, they felt hopeful and much more trusting as they prepared to enter the election of a new provincial.

As a result of this group experience of forgiveness and healing, the men seemed able to dream and to hope again as a group. As a group, they had allowed themselves to experience and acknowledge before God and one another their brokenness, their sinfulness, and their powerlessness to overcome obstacles to unity. In addition, they were able to ask for God's help to become reconciled to one another.

I suspect that underlying many of the conflicts between Christians of goodwill are such acknowledged or unacknowledged negative feelings that we have never thought to bring to God for healing in some communal fashion. In our churches, there are many deep divisions. God wants to help us become reconciled. Perhaps the thoughts here occasioned by reflection on communal discernment can be useful as we look for ways to allow God to bring about such reconciliation.

Let me end these chapters on forgiveness with a poem by Susan Kay called "Would You Do the Same Today?" She wrote it on the anniversary of the terrorist attacks on the World Trade Center and the Pentagon of September 11, 2001.

September 11, 2002

Jesus, you got nailed by terror and evil
long before we did,
You looked it in the eye—prayed—
and refused to hold your love at bay.
Have you thought of a better way?
Or would you do the same today?

I picked up a prayer card after mass.
It has a picture of a golden cross
hanging beneath an American flag.
On the back is a prayer
    —a prayer for protection from terrorists
    —a prayer that God help us work for justice
    —a prayer that God be with us
and with our troops
and with our allies.

There is no prayer for our enemies
Maybe that's not something we hear
from golden crosses
hanging beneath American flags
    —or maybe there just wasn't room.

But they say that is what was heard
from a wooden cross

hanging beneath darkened skies

    —prayer for those who hung you there
    —prayer for those who watched and laughed
    —prayer for those who ran and hid
    —prayer for those who only watch and weep.

Jesus, can you kindle that love in us?
Can you teach us to pray?
Even when we can't—especially when we can't—
Jesus, keep showing us you can.
Hate came out of a clear blue sky
and slammed into our buildings.
Hate laughed in your face
and slammed through your hands.
We try to bomb the hell out of it.
You looked it in the eye—prayed—
and refused to hold your love at bay.

    Have you thought of a better way?
    Or would you do the same today?[35]

9

Compassion of Heart, Global in Scope

The Lord is compassionate and merciful.
—JAMES 5:11

In "Compassion and Peace," Edward Niziolek, SJ, writes:

Does it matter that two lovers
commit suicide on some hidden back road?

Does it matter that a mother and
her three children are bombed to death
to leave her husband alone in the world?

Does it really matter that some old spinsters
die in an abandoned apartment with rodents
all around?

Does it matter that a ninety year old
debilitated couple feel deep pain and
hurt from seeing the other's decrepitude?

Does it matter that we see the pain, hurt,
insurmountable anguish in another and
can do nothing about it?

Does it make any difference whether
we look out at the world through
the eyes of peace or compassion?[36]

Clearly, Niziolek has been deeply touched by events he has witnessed or read about. And he raises the heartrending question, Does compassion really make a difference in the grander scheme? In this chapter, let's focus on the fact that the God revealed in the Bible is a God of compassion—and what this means for us and for our world.

Compassion Means "Womb Love"

The Hebrew word translated as compassion, *rachamim*, is related to the Hebrew word for "womb." Compassion is womb love. It's the kind of love a mother demonstrates when she risks herself for her child. Compassion is defined by a deep feeling of empathy and love for another and the willingness to risk oneself for the sake of the other. When we hear God described in the Old Testament as a merciful God or as full of mercy, the word *mercy* or its cognates usually translates *rachamim*, for example, in Exodus 34:6: "The LORD, the LORD, / a God merciful and gracious." God has such womb love for the human family that God risks self for us. For example, God risks our noncooperation. And every time God forgives us, the risk is that we will once again break God's heart. Most important, God takes the risk of becoming a human being for love of us wayward, often inhuman humans, and suffers the consequences. What does this attribute of God mean for us, who are created in the image of God?

In Luke's Gospel, a lawyer tests Jesus by asking what he must do to inherit eternal life. Jesus asks him about the law, and the lawyer cites the great commandment: love of God and love of neighbor. The story continues:

> But wanting to justify himself, he asked Jesus, "And who is my neighbor?" Jesus replied, "A man was going down from Jerusalem to Jericho, and fell into the hands of robbers, who stripped him, beat him, and went away, leaving him half dead. Now by chance a priest was going down that road; and when he saw him, he passed by on the other side. So likewise a Levite, when he came to the place and saw him, passed by on the other side. But a Samaritan while traveling came near him; and when he saw him, he was moved with pity. He went to him and

bandaged his wounds, having poured oil and wine on them. Then he put him on his own animal, brought him to an inn, and took care of him. The next day he took out two denarii, gave them to the innkeeper, and said, 'Take care of him; and when I come back, I will repay you whatever more you spend.' Which of these three, do you think, was a neighbor to the man who fell into the hands of the robbers?" He said, "The one who showed him mercy." Jesus said to him, "Go and do likewise." (Luke 10:29–37)

The story shows us three people created in the image of God, and their reactions to a fellow human being in trouble. The two Jewish religious leaders pass by their fellow Jew who has been mugged and robbed on a very dangerous road. Because they are made in God's image, we can presume that their hearts were stirred at least a little to help this man. But they did not act on this stirring of the heart. Perhaps they were afraid that they themselves would be mugged and robbed, or even that the man on the side of the road was part of a gang of robbers trying to lure them to stop. Perhaps they feared that he was dead and that they would be contaminated by touching him; touching a dead man would make them ritually unclean and, therefore, unable to perform their religious duties. At any rate they passed up the opportunity to help a fellow Jew in trouble. But the Samaritan, "moved with pity" (compassion or womb love) for this poor Jew, stopped to take care of him. He risked being mugged and robbed himself, and he lost time and money to care for this man who, we need to remind ourselves, belonged to an enemy people.

Our neighbor is any human being who needs our help. God is moved with compassion, womb love, for any human being in need; those of us made in God's image are also moved with such compassion. But we must act on those movements of compassion to live out our destiny as God's sons and daughters. When we act on them, we transform real-life situations in ways that are often hidden from our eyes.

Such movements happen to us every day, don't they? A fellow worker asks to speak to me in the midst of a busy day. I feel myself torn between getting my work done and listening to her. On my way to work, a beggar asks for money because he's out of work. Do I stop to speak to him or even make eye contact with him, or do I avoid any contact because I need to get to work? I notice an elderly neighbor shoveling snow with difficulty as I leave for an errand. I am moved to go over to see if I can help, but the errand needs to get done. I am asked to write a letter to or call my congressional representative about the plight of people in our district without health insurance. I am moved by the plight of these people, but I also think of the time involved in writing or calling. On the way to a concert, I see a woman trip and injure her knee. I am moved to stop and help, but then I might be late for the concert.

You can add your own experiences to these; they happen all the time. I believe that God's spirit dwelling in our hearts prompts such movements of compassion. I'm not saying that every time we feel such movements we must act on them in order to be the neighbor Jesus wants us to be. But please reflect on what these movements within you might mean. When these situations arise, how will your responses reflect your friendship with God and your cooperation with God in renewing this world?

Compassion Makes Its Mark on the World

Let me give you three examples that show how the way we respond to these interior movements toward compassion changes situations.

Jesus touched an untouchable.

We begin with Jesus. "A leper came to him begging him, and kneeling he said to him, 'If you choose, you can make me clean.' Moved with pity, Jesus stretched out his hand and touched him, and said to him, 'I do choose. Be made clean!' Immediately the leprosy left him, and he was made clean" (Mark 1:40–42). The Greek word translated as "pity" here has something to do with the gut; it is a gut-wrenching sympathy, possibly tinged with anger. (It is, by the way, the same Greek word translated as "pity" in the story of the Good Samaritan and used to translate the Hebrew word for compassion in the Greek version of the Hebrew Bible.) Jesus is moved with gut or womb love by this stranger's plight. It leads him to stop what he is doing and to pay attention to the leper.

In Jesus' time, lepers were exiled from the community because it was thought that the disease was passed on by physical contact. Moreover, touching a leper made one ritually unclean. So Jesus took a great risk in touching the man. He could have gotten the disease himself, and those who saw him act in this crazy way would have considered him unclean. But he did touch the man—and in doing so brought the man back into the community with unknown consequences in the world of his time, both for Jesus and for the cured leper.

This story, by the way, can be seen as a metaphor for what God does in becoming human; God takes the risk of becoming infected by our sinfulness. God "made him to be sin," as Paul wrote in 2 Corinthians 5:21. Even though Jesus was sinless, this does not mean that he was not continually engulfed in a sinful world, tempted by its allure, and in that sense contaminated by it. Out of compassion for us, God took a great risk.

A Hutu calls a Tutsi her son.

In his terrifying journey to escape the genocide of Tutsis in Burundi, a young medical student named Deogratias had come to what seemed the end of his strength and hope. As he woke from sleep, he spotted a woman walking away from another group of refugees and coming toward him. He was terrified but had lost the will even to run away.

It turned out that she was a Hutu who knew that he was afraid she would want to kill him. "But," she said, "I'm a woman and I'm a mother." She persuaded him to get up and to come with her. As they neared the border of Rwanda, she told him to say not that he was a Tutsi but that he was her son. Later when the Hutu militia threatened Deogratias, she risked her own life, declaring that he was her son. He never saw her again.

Deogratias eventually made it to New York City, where, after incredible hardships, he was able to finish college, go to medical school, and found a clinic back in Burundi in a village where his parents had finally settled, a village whose population is mainly Hutu. This nameless Hutu woman had compassion on a fellow human being with tremendous consequences for the future of the world.[37]

A priest befriends an inmate.

Some years ago, I received a phone call from a former student who had become a prison chaplain. Darrell Jones, the prisoner we met in chapter 5, had asked the chaplain if he knew someone who was a religious person and a psychologist; he wanted to correspond with someone like that about some things in his life. George asked me if I would be willing to receive the first letter from him. I hesitated, wondering what

I was letting myself in for; I had never engaged in such a correspondence and was involved in a number of enterprises that filled my day. But I also felt moved to respond positively because I fit the profile of what the prisoner wanted, and I wanted to help in any way I could. The latter movement won out.

Darrell was at a crossroads in his life in prison and needed to write to someone who might help. I responded to his letters as best I could. After a few letters back and forth, he nearly broke my heart when he wondered whether I knew that he was African American. Darrell considers me the kind of father he never had and credits our letters and visits as a lifesaving thing for him. I consider him a friend who would do anything he could for me.

Before Darrell met me, he had already met God and was doing what he could to care for others, especially his three sons who were at risk of getting into trouble on the streets of Boston. But as a result of my response to George's question, something happened to both of us that has had an effect on the larger world in sometimes profound ways. Darrell continues to work for an end to violence in the neighborhood where he and his sons lived and for changes in the prison that will help prisoners return to their community as more responsible citizens. I am different also and now try to do what I can to get Darrell's message out to others in the hope that more people will try to move their neighborhoods toward becoming more just and caring for all. As a result of this encounter, I have had to look back at my life and ask God's forgiveness for those times when I did not respond positively when the stirrings of compassion rose in me.

A neighbor offers her presence.

Another example comes from a widow whom I see for spiritual direction and who has given me permission to tell her story. I will call her Mary.

One morning as Mary left her house dressed for the gym, she noticed an ambulance at her neighbors' house. Her first impulse was to go on to the gym, but then she felt a stirring of compassion for her elderly neighbors, who had been good to her when her husband was dying. With some reluctance, she went back into her house, changed clothes, and went over to the neighbors' house. The husband had had a seizure during the night. Mary talked with the wife until the ambulance was ready to take her husband to the hospital and then drove her to the hospital. Mary ended up staying with the woman for hours, talking with her and comforting her as she met with the doctors and nurses who had the difficult task of announcing the husband's death. Together they read the medical examiner's pronouncement, prayed with her priest who came to be with her, and embraced family members as they arrived at the hospital. Mary drove her home after her final good-bye to her husband.

Afterward Mary felt that she had been with Jesus throughout the ordeal. Later in the day, she dropped in at the neighbor's house to see if there was anything she could do. The wife smiled through her tears and said, "I called 911, and God sent me you." Mary was overwhelmed with gratitude at God's goodness to her and to this woman whom she loved. A part of the world was changed for the better by her act of compassion.

When we act on movements of compassion for our fellow human beings, we are God's instruments in changing some part of our world for the better. Simone Weil, the French philosopher who died at a young age during World War II, once wrote: "God is absent from the world, except in the existence of those in whom His love is alive. Therefore they ought to be present in the world through compassion. Their compassion is the visible presence of God here below."[38]

We may never know the effects of our actions, but we can be sure that we are cooperating with God in moving the world toward the dream of a new heaven and a new earth.

We Dare Move toward an Ideal World

In his Gifford Lectures of 1953–54 at the University of Glasgow, Scottish philosopher John Macmurray developed the theory that persons are defined by their relationships and that the only way persons can achieve what they want and what God wants is by trying to overcome their fears of one another so that they can care for one another. Macmurray summarizes the ideal that God intends in this pithy sentence: "It is a universal community of persons in which each cares for all the others and no one for himself." A new earth, indeed.[39]

Of course, the ideal is never achieved; our real world is both the old earth and the new earth and will be until the end of history. In reality, fears for ourselves bedevil all of us; hence, all of us tend to care for ourselves more often than we care for others. But the spirit of God moves us toward this ideal. When compassion for another human being moves us and we act on that movement, then, for that moment at least, we have forgotten ourselves and are caring for the other, risky though it may be. When we act on such movements, we change a part of our world for the better with consequences we cannot know. Of course, when we turn away from movements of compassion because of fear or any other motive, we also affect a part of our world with consequences we cannot know. The choice is ours.

Now, remember that we are presenting an ideal. What Jesus is asking of us should not make us scrupulous and anxious. In fact, if we do become scrupulous and anxious, we can be sure that we are not being moved by the spirit of God, because such feelings lead us to more and more self-absorption. After I became aware of how much good came of my responding to Darrell, I looked back at my life and asked God's forgiveness for those times when I did not act on the stirrings of compassion. I did not experience God as wagging a finger at me, wanting me to wallow in self-con-demnation. Rather, I felt a sense of freedom to be able to see my life truthfully and know that I was forgiven. I felt grati-tude that I had been given the grace to respond positively to Darrell. I'm sure that Mary would say the same.

God knows our weakness, our human propensity to fail in this divine friendship, but God still tries to bring us back to being our best selves. God's truth telling is for our good and for the advancement of the dream, not for our fixation on guilt and punishment. We can and must rue our sin-ful past, but it is not God's desire that such ruefulness lead us away from caring for others, which fixation on our sins will do.

Compassion Matters at Any Level

But what about Edward Niziolek's haunting question cited at the beginning of this chapter? "Does it matter that we see the pain, hurt, / insurmountable anguish in another and / can do nothing about it. / Does it make any difference whether / we look out at the world through / the eyes of peace or compassion?" We often run into people who are suffering, and we feel moved to compassion but do not have the time or wherewithal to do anything to help. When we read the newspapers or watch television, we witness hor-rors that move us to compassion for those who are hurt, but we feel helpless to do anything about the situation. Do such movements of compassion have an effect on the world, or do they merely burden us with grief to no avail?

As I pondered this question, I thought of what God seems to endure all the time. God is compassion itself, we believe, filled with womb love for all who live on this earth. Every day, God is present to even greater horrors than any of us have witnessed and seems powerless to change the circumstances. Tectonic plates shift, and a huge tsunami wipes out a quarter of a million people, leaving millions of others grieving and without sustenance. Can you imagine God shrugging it off as just another minor blip in the ongoing process of creation? I cannot. I believe that our movements of helpless compassion are a pale reflection of God's reaction to such horrors. Moreover, suffering people often find God's presence and care immensely consoling, even though they know that God cannot change the circumstances.

Many of the horrors we read about in the newspapers or see on television are caused by human blunders and sin. Again, God cannot force us to be intelligent, moral, and humane. God keeps the world in existence as human beings perpetrate almost unimaginable horrors, including the horror on Golgotha two thousand years ago. God's compassion is always trying to draw human hearts away from such heinous acts, but very often we don't pay attention. How do you imagine God reacting? I believe that God keeps hoping that we will turn from our inhuman ways, keeps trying to move us in this direction, and mourns for and tries to comfort the victims of our inhumanity.

The Scriptures speak of God's anger at such situations but also of God's willingness to forgive and to relent from venting that anger. God's compassion does not mean that wrongdoing is not judged as wrongdoing. But God's compassion does seem to offer all of us the hope and the grace of changed hearts. God's compassion has an effect on the world because it produces such conversions and most likely has prevented even greater horrors than what have already occurred.

Could it be that our feelings of compassion—even though they seem futile at times because we can do nothing to change events—converge with God's compassion and thus contribute to the positive energies on this planet? Could it be that our compassion and repentance have at least as much of an effect on the world as do the negative energies of hatred, intolerance, and unforgiveness?

Simone Weil wrote movingly about the need of compassion for the future of our world. At its heart, she believes, compassion means "to give one's attention to a sufferer," which "is a very rare and difficult thing; it is almost a miracle; it is a miracle." She continued:

The love of our neighbor in all its fullness simply means being able to say to him: "What are you going through?" It is a recognition that the sufferer exists, not only as a

unit in a collection, or a specimen from the social cate-
gory labeled "unfortunate," but as a man, exactly like us,
who was one day stamped with a special mark of afflic-
tion. For this reason it is enough, but it is indispensable,
to know how to look at him in a certain way.[40]

Her description of this attitude comes down to this: to look
with attention and care at the person without worrying
about oneself. This kind of looking is what I have called
contemplative; we forget ourselves and pay attention to the
other in all that other's uniqueness. What this look does is to
make the other feel a part of the human family, even when
we cannot do anything to change the circumstances. With
this look, we are living out our God-likeness; we are acting
like God, who looks in this way at all of us suffering and
wayward human beings.

Try to imagine a world in which many people looked
in this way at those in need and asked of them the simple
question, "What are you going through?" There would be
a contagion of compassion. We could not help but want to
pass on the gift we have received. In fact, isn't this what
we believe happens with holy people, that they exude such
a sense of God's compassion that they attract other people
and even animals? St. Francis of Assisi drew human beings
and animals to him as honey draws flies, and many were
changed by the encounter.

In my own religious order, the Jesuits, I have noted how holiness often spread like a virus through its early members. Ignatius of Loyola, for example, became a roommate of two other students at the University of Paris, Pierre Favre and Francis Xavier. Pierre and Francis were drawn to make the Spiritual Exercises under Ignatius's direction. The three, along with seven other companions from Paris, became the founders of the Society of Jesus; Ignatius and Xavier were canonized, and Pierre beatified. The Jesuit brother Alphonsus Rodríguez, the doorkeeper in the Jesuit school at Majorca in Spain, befriended the scholastic Peter Claver and encouraged him in his desire to become a missionary in South America, where he spent his life attending to the needs of African slaves who were brought in ships to the port of Cartagena. Both have been canonized.

Profound compassion that leads to the look Weil describes is tremendously attractive and does change the world in ways we cannot fully fathom. So if we allow ourselves to grow in friendship with God, we will have an effect on the world—even when it seems that we cannot change the events in it.

So, to Edward Niziolek's poignant question, I would say this: it does matter a great deal that we react with deep feelings of compassion for the sorrows of so many people. And I am grateful to Niziolek for allowing himself to feel so deeply for people even though he feels helpless to do anything about their plight. In fact, just by writing and going to great lengths to publish his poem, Niziolek has had an impact on the world. As more and more of us allow ourselves to experience the suffering of others and react with compassion, we will begin to do what we can in our respective homes and cities to change the way things are. It does make a difference whether we look at the world through the eyes of compassion or of peace.

10

Life with Others

Love one another as I have loved you.
—JOHN 15:12

We are embedded in many different groups: family, neighborhood, parish, city, state, country, and world. In fact, we find our identity as persons only in and through our participation in such groups. What does friendship with God mean for how we engage with others in these different communities or groups of people? We have already dealt with some answers to this question in earlier chapters. However, I want to take it up more explicitly here.

God Sees the Entire Human Family

First, let's remember that God's interest is not in individuals alone; God creates our world so that we human beings might become friends of God, of one another, and in some real way, of the whole of creation. God has a stake in how we live in the communities into which we are born, work, worship, and find some ordered civic, social, and cultural life. Wherever we are, we are on holy ground because God is present and active, working to bring about the divine dream. "Sacred" and "secular" are our categories, not God's.

As we saw in chapter 4, we are called to be friends of God wherever life places us. God wants our cooperation to tend the garden that is our planet and to move every community in which we live toward the ideal of God's own life of friendship, mutual love, and care. Since the resurrection of Jesus and Pentecost, Christians are called and empowered to live toward the new heavens and the new earth that God began some two thousand years ago, to be signs that the rule of God has already begun. Compassion, care, and forgiveness are the hallmarks of God and thus of those who are called to live in this world as friends and images of God.

God's spirit prompts every human being to overcome the fears that lead to self-concern so that we might be more able to care for our planet and for those who live with us. Every day we can ask God to help us become less focused on our own needs and turf and thus more attentive to the needs of others. Like the worker priest Jerome Strozzi in the novel *Eternity, My Beloved*, we can pray every day for those we will meet: "Through me let her find what she is looking for. Let me try to be the other, and bring to life in myself what, in spite of appearances, is true in her." Strozzi was the compassionate heart of God in the red-light district of Paris. We are invited to be the compassionate heart of God in our homes, our work sites, our parishes, and our cities. Just imagine how different family, work, and civic life would be if every Christian were to act more or less consistently in this way!

The description of the earliest Christian community in Jerusalem gives us an idea of what that might be like. Let me repeat that text here:

> All who believed were together and had all things in common; they would sell their possessions and goods and distribute the proceeds to all, as any had need. Day by day, as they spent much time together in the temple, they broke bread at home and ate their food with glad and generous hearts, praising God and having the goodwill of all the people. And day by day the Lord added to their number those who were being saved (Acts 2:44–47).

Our friendship with God can show itself powerfully in ordinary life. Because of the compassion this friendship develops within, people have faced ruthless power without fear, have been able to forgive the seemingly unforgivable, and have risked their lives and reputations for the greater good. The presence and action of the Spirit make possible the actions we see as heroic, and often people carry out such heroism without even knowing that God's spirit was moving them. For example, the Burundian Deogratias (whom we met in chapter 9) met another example of God's compassion in a baggage handler at Kennedy Airport who was asked to translate Deogratias's French by customs officials. His name was Muhammad, a Muslim from Senegal, who befriended Deogratias and helped him through customs and then took him under his wing to get him started in New York City. The action of God's spirit is not limited to Christians; God's spirit touches the hearts of every human being.[41]

In the preface to the second Eucharistic Prayer for Masses of Reconciliation, the priest prays in our name:

> In the midst of conflict and division,
> we know it is you
> who turn our minds to thoughts of peace.
> Your Spirit changes our hearts:
> enemies begin to speak to one another,
> those who were estranged join hands in friendship,
> and nations seek the way of peace together.
> Your Spirit is at work
> when understanding puts an end to strife,
> when hatred is quenched by mercy,
> and vengeance gives way to forgiveness.
> For this we should never cease
> to thank and praise you.

This prayer speaks of the real-world results of the presence and action of God's spirit in ordinary people like us. It tells us something about how, as friends of God, we might live as family members and citizens of both church and state.

In *Surprised by Hope*, the Anglican bishop of Durham (England), N. T. Wright, writes that our task as a church is to work for God's kingdom, for the new heavens and new earth that God has already begun with the resurrection of Jesus. What does this mean for us? Wright enumerates some of the actions that fulfill that task:

> Every act of love, gratitude, and kindness; every work of art or music inspired by the love of God and delight in the beauty of his creation; every minute spent teaching a severely handicapped child to read or to walk; every act of care and nurture, of comfort and support, for one's fellow human beings and for that matter one's fellow nonhuman creatures; and of course every prayer, all Spirit-led teaching, every deed that spreads the gospel, builds up the church, embraces and embodies holiness rather than corruption, and makes the name of Jesus honored in the world—all of this will find its way, through the resurrecting power of God, into the new creation that God will one day make.[42]

Because God's spirit is at work in everyone, we can hope to find some of these same actions everywhere, not only among Christians. What nobler or more urgent task could we have?

Love Faces the Conflict of Beliefs

In chapters 3 and 4, we noted that God and God's relation to the world are what they are irrespective of our beliefs. However, it is important for us to recognize that belief systems are at the heart of our behavior; what we believe and what we cherish move us to act. These beliefs and loves have more to do with our hearts than our minds—which brings us back to the idea that we need to develop hearts and minds more in tune with what God intends.

But the people of this world differ profoundly in their beliefs about the nature of the world, the purpose of life, the existence of God, and what constitutes a good life. Even those who believe that God exists differ among themselves on many issues. Different beliefs lead to conflicting ways of life in the same country or region, even in the same family. How do adult friends of God negotiate their way in this thicket of different ways of life and thus contribute to God's dream for our world and every citizen's desire to live at peace?

As we try to answer this question, let's remember that all of us have undeveloped areas of mind and heart. We grope for answers to the great questions that plague our world, and we do so with minds and hearts not totally in tune with God's dream. So even though our beliefs are about the world and what God dreams for it, our underdeveloped minds and hearts may lead us astray not only about what God wants in this concrete situation but also about how we achieve what God wants.

As a parent, I may believe that my twenty-three-year-old son is making a big mistake in considering marriage to a Jewish woman he loves. As I think of talking with him, it might be wise to ask God's help to see myself and my son as God sees us. Am I being overprotective of my son, feeling that I should be able to keep him from making mistakes? Am I influenced by prejudices about interreligious marriages and by my limited knowledge of how such marriages turn out? Do I have legitimate concerns that God would want me to raise? If I do ask for God's help in this way, I may be more able to talk to my son about my concerns with attention to his mind and heart and a desire to help him make the best decision he can. My son is not the only one who can learn and grow from the conversation.

Things get more complex when it comes to dealing with conflicting beliefs outside the family—at work, in church, or in civic life. Today, many beliefs and patterns of behavior are under scrutiny in the culture at large. Because of modern technology and economies, our various communities have become increasingly intertwined. We are aware, probably more than our grandparents were, of how the life of each person on this planet is affected by every other life. Yet each of us tends to think and feel locally rather than globally about what we need and desire. The great Speaker of the U.S. House of Representatives, Thomas "Tip" O'Neill, used to say that all politics is local. Our local ties, therefore, color our reactions to conflicts of interest much more than our ties to all humanity and to the environment. Hence, all of us are biased. If we can keep this in mind when facing those who disagree with us, we will approach them with more willingness to listen, attentively and respectfully, to their point of view. In the process, we might able to help one another overcome our local prejudices. "How does God view this opponent and me?" might be a good question to ask as we approach a community conflict.

Also, our belief systems are vulnerable because they are no longer supported by a monolithic culture or religion. In his monumental study *A Secular Age*, the Canadian philosopher Charles Taylor traces the historical trajectory that has led, in the Western world,

> from a society in which it was virtually impossible not to believe in God, to one in which faith, even for the staunchest believer, is one human possibility among others. I may find it inconceivable that I would abandon my faith, but there are others, including possibly some very close to me, whose way of living I cannot in all honesty just dismiss as depraved, or blind, or unworthy, who have no faith (at least not in God, or the transcendent).[43]

In other words, everyone's belief system is vulnerable because almost everyone knows people of goodwill who do not believe as he or she does.

What happens in such a situation? When beliefs are shared in a community or country, it can seem irrational or insane to doubt, but when beliefs are not shared, as is the case today, then each of us is prey to doubt. In a way, the modern predicament can be seen as a blessing; it makes it clear that faith is precisely faith, trust that what we believe is true. "Now faith is the assurance of things hoped for, the conviction of things not seen," as the letter to the Hebrews puts it (Hebrews 11:1). There is no knockdown argument that guarantees our faith in God. However, because most of us find it hard to live by such faith, we become anxious when doubts are aroused by living in this secular age. We doubt our beliefs and look for assurance.

Where do we turn? For some of us, a book such as *A Secular Age*, written by a very learned and believing Roman Catholic philosopher, provides some security of faith. But any security might blind us to the fact that our faith is rather fragile and endangered.

Also, we might wall ourselves off from views that conflict with our own by listening only to those who believe as we do and writing off as foolish or self-serving or immoral the views of those who disagree. The spread of fundamentalisms of every sort in the past century, from those of totalitarian political movements such as fascism or communism to various religious fundamentalist movements in almost every country in the world, may be traceable, at least in part, to the vulnerability of all beliefs in this secular age. The strident

anger that accompanies so many religious and political con-
troversies may also be an attempt to ward off doubt. Even
the sometimes-vitriolic anger against all religions that finds
expression in best-selling books by atheists or agnostics may
be a sign that they, too, suffer from the vulnerability of all
belief systems. (Strange to say, atheism is as much a belief as
is theism; there is no more a knockdown argument for the
nonexistence of God than there is for God's existence.) If we
are aware of how vulnerable all our beliefs are, we may be
more compassionate toward ourselves and those who differ
with us as we try to work together to improve our world.

We might stir up some compassion by reflecting on the
time when Jesus went aside to be alone with his disciples.
A crowd beat them to the spot. Mark (6:34) writes: "As he
went ashore, he saw a great crowd; and he had compassion
for them, because they were like sheep without a shepherd;
and he began to teach them many things." We can remind
ourselves that Jesus has the same compassion now toward all
of us as we try to work out acceptable solutions to the conflicts that permeate life in an unpredictable world.

Friendship Leads to Respect

What does friendship with God teach us about how to
manage value and belief conflicts in our various circles of
community? Well, we can take our cue from God—our
friend—who does not coerce us but who tries to draw us

into becoming our best selves. Just as we learn forgiveness from how God forgives us, so we can learn from God's way of friendship and try to befriend all those we meet, even those who differ from us. Jesus once said: "Come to me, all you that are weary and are carrying heavy burdens, and I will give you rest. Take my yoke upon you, and learn from me; for I am gentle and humble in heart, and you will find rest for your souls. For my yoke is easy, and my burden is light" (Matthew 11:28–30). As we try to convince others of our vision of what God wants in this world, let's remember that Jesus addressed those words to them as well as to us. After all, those who oppose us often are acting on beliefs that they hold as religiously as we hold ours. If everyone is called to friendship with God, then all people we meet, even those who oppose our cherished beliefs about how human beings should live in this world, are the focus of God's great love.

When we demonize another child of God, even one who commits heinous crimes, we use the tactics of the enemy of human nature, not the tactics of God. In Greek Orthodox spirituality, there is a story about a monk who showed such admirable restraint when two other monks abused him that his elder, the Abba Theodoros, asked him how he maintained his tranquility. The monk responded, "Am I to pay attention to these animals?" Theodoros went back to his cell and wept that this monk's heart was so perverted. Father Maximos, who told this story to Kyriacos Markides, went on to explain:

For monks, or for everybody else for that matter, such thoughts are inexcusable. We must never see our fellow human beings as anything other than the image of God. Monks are expected to see the image of God when they encounter any human being. We must never see human beings either as demons, donkeys, dogs, or anything else, regardless of what they do to us or what their behavior is like.[44]

One thing that friendship with God leads to is respect for all human beings—all made in God's image—no matter how much we may disagree with or even abhor their moral or political choices.

There Are More People with Us Than We Think

Friends of God are invited to live without fear, trusting that God will work with our best efforts and those of others. God is creating the new heavens and the new earth at every moment, and in spite of what it sometimes seems, God's dream *will* come about. Also, the more we grow in faith in the movement of the Spirit in others, the more we will look for those movements, even in people who seem entrenched in positions opposed to ours.

Recall the story in 2 Kings where the king of Aram, enraged against the prophet Elisha, surrounds Elisha's town with a large army. Elisha's servant cries in dismay, even despair:

"Alas, master! What shall we do?" He replied, "Do not be afraid, for there are more with us than there are with them." Then Elisha prayed: "O LORD, please open his eyes that he may see." So the LORD opened the eyes of the servant, and he saw; the mountain was full of horses and chariots of fire around Elisha. (2 Kings 6:15–17)

In our civic and religious contentions, we are not dealing with armies, but often believers become discouraged, feeling that we are in the minority on major issues of public policy and morality. We should not forget that, because of the outpouring of God's Spirit, "there are more with us" than we think. We will find civility, forgiveness, compassion, and concern for justice for all people in the oddest places. And if we treat others with civility and compassion, we may find that they respond in kind; then we can move forward to search for a mutually satisfying solution to our disagreements.

As I was writing this section, I began reading a remarkable book by Rebecca Solnit, aptly titled *A Paradise Built in Hell*, on how ordinary people actually act in times of disaster. The prevailing wisdom is that, in any disaster, people will panic, act selfishly, and engage in random violence and looting. As a result, when governments prepare for such emergencies, their preoccupation is on military and police readiness to deal with a citizenry run amok. But, according to Solnit, and many of the sociologists who have studied how people actually respond in disasters, governments often make things worse rather than better. The media, also taken in by the prevailing wisdom, play up rumors of looting and rape as though these were the only stories worth telling during a disaster. And in fact, most of the rumors turn out to be false. In many cases, panic, fueled by prevailing wisdom and such rumors, leads to making the victims of natural or manmade disasters into the enemy, with disastrous results.

Sociological studies of disasters, however, show that ordinary people most often do not panic when a disaster occurs; rather, they become innovative, form small communities, and help others, often at some cost to themselves. Solnit focuses on five great disasters: the earthquake in San Francisco in 1906; the explosion of a munitions ship in Halifax harbor during the World War I; the earthquake in Mexico City on September 19, 1985; the terrorist attack on the twin towers of the World Trade Center on September 11, 2001; and Hurricane Katrina in New Orleans in 2005. In all cases, ordinary people typically rose to the occasion and exhibited extraordinary willingness to help their neighbors and even strangers, sometimes at some risk to themselves. Just one example of many comes from the terrorist attack on the World Trade Center on September 11, 2001: a young immigrant Pakistani, Usman Farman, was running from the cloud of ash from the falling towers when he fell down. Then:

A Hasidic Jewish man came up to him, took into his hand the pendant with an Arabic prayer on it that Farman wore, and then "with a deep Brooklyn accent he said, 'Brother if you don't mind, there is a cloud of glass coming at us. Grab my hand, let's get the hell out of here.' He was the last person I would ever have thought to help me. If it weren't for him, I probably would have been engulfed in shattered glass and debris."[45]

As I read the book, I realized that under rather appalling circumstances ordinary people more often than not act as people truly made in God's image. The spirit of God was more powerfully present than the spirit expected by prevailing opinion. As we engage in efforts to bring civil societies more in line with God's dream for our world, we might keep in mind that there are more with us than with "them" and remain open to the possibility that all of us would rather live in a society that treasures life and community over individual rights alone.

Jesus went to his death on the cross with faith and trust that God would write straight with the crooked line of his crucifixion, would prevail through this seeming defeat. If we hold to such faith and trust, we can live without fear, doing our best to cooperate with God's dream, thus working in harmony with God's intention and becoming part of God's healing presence.

God's Friends Work toward a New Earth

We still need to address how believers work with others to achieve a society that conforms to God's hopes. The issues we face in this section may remind some readers of Augustine's grappling with similar issues in the massive work of his old age, *The City of God*. Robert Louis Wilken notes that for Augustine, the phrase "city of God" "designated a company of men and women and angels who are united in their love of God," whereas the earthly city designated "the social and political community that exercises dominion over human beings." According to Augustine, citizens of the city of God are also citizens of the earthly city and must play their part in it. In this, he is articulating what it means to be a human created by God and living in this world of earthly cities.[46]

Augustine seems to equate the church with the city of God. However, not even the church is a society that attains complete union in "their love of God." All human societies, even religious ones, are flawed. We who live in families, churches, cities, and other institutions are still in thrall to old-earth values even while those of the new earth pull us. No individual or community is immune from the two pulls. The reign or rule of God, while present, is still not fully achieved. This is the reality of our world. Still, we are called to work with God toward the new earth.

This section of the book has been very difficult to write. Only after numerous failed attempts did I realize that the only way forward was to hold fast to the image of friendship with God and to write only from that standpoint. The other attempts failed either because I was hedging my bets so as not to offend readers or because I was overwhelmed by the complexities of the issues involved. In neither case was I writing as a friend of God. So I resolved to deal with one or two difficult issues, asking God to help me to write as a friend.

Two Issues, Two Examples

How, as a friend of God, do I help change the climate that seems to allow abortion on demand in the United States? As I imagined a discussion with God about this issue, a great sadness came over me: sadness for babies killed, for the many women who have felt cornered and saw no other way out, for the many women and men and their helpers in the abortion process for whom abortion was nothing more than a normal medical procedure, for doctors and nurses who performed abortions reluctantly to save determined women from unsafe procedures, for the many men and women filled with guilt because of a past abortion. The list went on. It also came to me that to reduce abortions a society would have to do everything it could to ensure health care for pregnant women and young children; to improve living standards for the poor; to protect women more effectively from exploitation and rape, including marital rape. We would have to change the culture of violence and of self-indulgence that makes abortion a likely alternative to care for the unborn.

What really happened as I thought about abortion? In God's presence, I became aware of how complex the issue is. What can a friend of God do to change the climate? Awareness of the complexities may allow us to engage, with more empathy, with those who disagree with us on this issue. Perhaps we can try to move the argument away from conflicting rights, whereby we put the unborn in opposition to pregnant women, to consideration of what a good society might look like for all of us. It goes without saying that, as friends of God, we must never demonize those who oppose our position. No matter how convinced I am that the preservation of unborn human life is an absolute moral duty, hasty dismissal of those with different viewpoints serves only to deepen and widen the impasse, making a change of climate more difficult. And those on both sides of this issue who seek dialogue will have to contend with cries of betrayal from those who see no other possibility than a clear win for their position.

How do I go about reducing the number of guns available in the United States? Again, as I imagined a discussion with God, I felt a great sadness for the many people, especially the young, killed by guns every day, for the families of those killed, for those who had inadvertently shot someone with a gun kept in the house for protection, for people so fearful of others that they felt the need to keep guns in their homes, for those twisted people who had so easily been able to get guns to go on killing sprees. As I pondered this issue in God's presence, I realized that I harbored some disdain for those who argue against any restriction on the sale of guns. With such disdain I could not engage with them in a way that might lead to a better society. This leads me to wonder how I can help more and more of my fellow citizens to envision a society in which guns are not considered necessary for our protection. How can we move together toward a society in which we are less afraid of one another?

Even in our present, not fully realized new earth, those of us who try to live as grown-up friends of God can ask God for the grace to try to engage in discussions with "the same mind . . . that was in Christ Jesus,"

> who, though he was in the form of God,
>   did not regard equality with God
>   as something to be exploited,
> but emptied himself,
>   taking the form of a slave,
>   being born in human likeness.
> And being found in human form,
>   he humbled himself
>   and became obedient to the point of death—
>   even death on a cross. (Philippians 2:5–8)

God has such humility, patience, and love for us. Let's beg God to help us act with a similar kind of humility, patience, and love for one another.

The trouble is, of course, that many of us do not give the other the benefit of the doubt. And, as the story of the Greek monk illustrates, this is true in places such as religious monasteries, where belief in God as the creator of all human beings is professed. Any honest history of Christianity shows how venality, greed, and the hunger for power have moved those who profess belief in Jesus more than humility, compassion, and forgiveness. So in any debate in the political, economic, or even religious arena on an issue over which the parties differ strongly, the imaginary scenes of honest and considerate discussion we have just contemplated are nowhere near the way things are. How does a friend of God act in such circumstances? Father Maximos would say that, no matter the provocation, the Christian is called to treat the other with the respect due another made in God's image. Treating another human being as anything less is wrong not just for a monk, but for any Christian. Friends of God show who they are by their works, by how they treat others, even those who treat them badly.

It might seem that we are back to the questions raised at the very beginning of this book about spirituality being too ethereal to have any impact on the real world. But recall what we reflected on in chapter 3—how inner attitudes make a palpable impact wherever we are. Again Father Maximos provides a hint as to the first step. In response to a question about the politically volatile division of Cyprus between Turks and Greeks, he said, "The first step toward a lasting peace with the Turks is to find peace within ourselves. Then outer peace will be its natural consequence." In Crete's volatile and dangerous quagmire, the Greek Cypriots had to begin with themselves, not demand change in the Turk Cypriots.[47]

Friendship with God can lead to such inner peace and to love even of our enemies; such a change of attitude on our part may lead the enemy's heart to genuine change as well.

Please don't misunderstand me. God pulls no punches in trying to move us toward being the humans we are created to be; there is no watering down of the demand for true holiness—we are indeed made in the image of God, who is holy. Just read how starkly Jesus puts these demands in the Sermon on the Mount in Matthew 5—7. As we try to convince others of how God wants the world to be organized, we need not pull our punches either. Friends of God will want to have an effect on civic and political life; they will want to leave this world in better shape than it was when they entered it. And they will have ideas and convictions, even passionate convictions, on how to do this. So they will let others know these convictions, for instance, that abortion kills the innocent or that war is immoral, without equivocation.

Jesus clearly wanted to change his world, and he did everything he could to bring people around to his way of living as people made in God's image. And Jesus had convictions—indeed, he died because of them. But how did he go about the work of changing the world? He ate and drank with tax collectors, prostitutes, and sinners, but also with scribes and Pharisees. Jesus excoriated the latter, but he never put them beyond the pale or refused to talk with them. He treated everyone as a son or daughter of God, and he refused to use the tactics of the Satan: fear, despair, anger, and coercion.

Pope Benedict XVI Calls Us to "Truth in Love"

In our attempts to influence others, we might take the lead of Pope Benedict XVI, whose recent encyclical letter *Truth in Love* is addressed not only to Catholic Christians but also to "all people of good will." He uses his position to call people to work together for a world more in conformity with God's desires. For Benedict, truth is very important, and truth is about what God wants for the created world. Benedict recognizes the enormity of the tasks facing humanity, but with faith in God's promises and presence, he tries to help us recognize what is for our common welfare.

But while speaking the truth about God's desires for the world, Benedict's tone is irenic and inviting (even if the letter is a daunting read), not condemnatory. In our own attempts to influence public policy, let us act as friends of God who loves "all things that exist, / and detest[s] none of the things that" he has made (Wisdom 11:24).[48]

In summarizing Augustine's position on the role of the church, Robert Wilkin writes:

> The church is not an instrument to achieve other ends than fellowship with God. It serves society by being unapologetically itself and by bearing witness to the justice that alone makes human community possible, the justice due God. The greatest gift the church can give . . . is a glimpse, however fleeting, of another city, where the angels keep "eternal festival."

The early Christians provided such a glimpse of God's nature. As we try to live as citizens of this world and as citizens of the new heaven and the new earth, let it be as believers in God, who wants friendship to prevail among all of God's children. If we try to live in this way, we cannot help but change our world for the better with unknown consequences for the future. Where we fail to live in this way, we also change our world with unknown consequences for the future, but clearly God will have to work overtime to undo the consequences. God has put the shape of the future in our hands.

11

Can We Say,
"We Have Enough"?

While I was finishing this book, our world was severely buf-
feted by an economic crisis that many likened to the depression of 1929. Unemployment soared, financial institutions
failed or were rescued by government bailouts, retirement
funds were decimated or entirely lost, and the piper's bill for
the rescue efforts looks to saddle generations to come. Then
the explosion of the BP deepwater oil well in the Gulf of
Mexico off Louisiana threatened the economy and ecology
along the whole Gulf Coast.

After I had finished the first draft of this book, I read
I.O.U.: Why Everyone Owes Everyone and No One Can Pay by
John Lanchester, a novelist who, in the course of research-
ing the crisis for a novel, found the story so riveting that he
decided to tell it. Lanchester helps the reader understand, at
least a little, some of the rather formidable economic con-
cepts that are bandied about these days to explain what happened. Bankers, economists, and politicians come in for a

fair share of the blame for what happened, but Lanchester makes it clear that most of us took part in the culture that enabled the crisis to unfold. In addition, the seemingly insatiable need for fuel for industries, automobiles, air conditioning, and so on, fueled the deepwater exploration for oil. Because the consequences of these crises will be with us for some time, and because all of us are enmeshed in the culture that enabled them, I decided to add this chapter.

According to Lanchester, the biggest contributor to the financial debacle was the unrealistic housing-market bubble fostered by governments and by banks that developed lending practices that seemed to remove all risk to the lenders themselves. He notes, writing of Great Britain, that the financial institutions did everything they could to entice people—and increasingly poor people—to get on the bandwagon and buy a house, even when they were very poor risks for being able to repay the mortgages.

> Although it's nice to reserve the blame for banks who made lending too easy, the great British public is just as much to blame. We grew obsessed with the price of our houses, felt richer than we should, borrowed money we didn't have, spent it on junk, and now that the downturn has happened—as it was bound to do—we want someone else to blame. Well boo hoo. Bankers are to blame, but we're to blame too. That's just as well, because we're the ones who are going to have to pay.[50]

For the effects of the oil-rig explosion, we are only too willing to blame BP, all oil companies, the U.S. government, and lax regulators, but Lanchester's "we're to blame, too" echoes in this disaster as well. All of us who demand cheap gasoline for our motor vehicles and cheap electricity to run our furnaces, air conditioners, and other utilities; who want to drive to malls and walk comfortably through them in heat or cold; who want access to any food no matter the season—all of us are to blame for the unsustainable lifestyle of wealthy countries that developing countries aspire to emulate.

Do these words hit home to you? We need to understand how so many of us were caught up in the roll of the good times, little registering that what goes up must come down eventually and that the good times for "us" were often at the expense of bad times for "them," mostly the poor, and for the environment.

Lanchester made me aware of two little-known predictions made in 1930 by the great economist John Maynard Keynes. In spite of the Depression, he predicted that the accumulation of wealth in Britain would continue to rise despite the Depression until, in 2030, the country would have wealth worth four to eight times what it was in 1930. He seems to be on target with this prediction but totally wrong with another. He also believed that when humanity reached this level of wealth, we would rid ourselves of greed and acquisitiveness. It's worth quoting Keynes at some length on this prediction.

We shall be able to afford to dare to assess the money-motive at its true value. The love of money as a possession—as distinguished from the love of money as a means to the enjoyments and realities of life—will be recognized for what it is, a somewhat disgusting morbidity, one of those semi-criminal, semi-pathological propensities which one hands over with a shudder to the specialists in mental disorder. All kinds of social customs and economic practices, affecting the distribution of wealth and economic rewards and penalties, which we now maintain at all costs, however distasteful and unjust they may be in themselves, because they are tremendously useful in promoting the accumulation of capital, we shall then be free, at last, to discard.[51]

"Keynes sure was wrong about all that," continues Lanchester. "The great increase in our prosperity over the last decades has caused no general sense that we should now slow down and reflect on where we are, who we are, and what we want from life."[52]

Our politicians, financiers, and other influential people aren't the only ones who need to reflect on "where we are, who we are, and what we want from life." Each one of us must reflect on the culture in which we are immersed. Even if, as Lanchester maintains, Western liberal democracies have been the most admirable societies that ever existed, they are not, as he also notes, perfect. Keynes's analysis of the money motive should give us pause. Don't we, too often, pay more regard to people who are wealthy; don't we tend to trust them more and want to emulate their lifestyle? Aren't we eager to have the latest automobile, the newest computer or cell phone, the largest and most advanced television screen?

When I was provincial of the New England province of the Jesuits, I rejoiced in the growth in the stock market because it meant the growth of our investments that funded formation of younger Jesuits and the care of older ones, as well as some of our apostolic efforts. Because of the growth, we were able to be more creative with our formation and health care, but I did not pause to reflect that some of this growth was a result of consumer culture that had gotten out of hand. In fact, I, too, hankered for a faster computer and a better printer. I noticed that if we could afford something new, we didn't often ask whether we really needed it. When we were in a direr financial position, we tended to be more careful about spending on the new. Keynes was wrong indeed. We needed an incentive to reflect on what drives our acquisitiveness.

Lanchester believes that the financial crisis is such a wake-up call. (The BP oil spill is another.) It is, he says, "capitalism's equivalent" of a benign heart attack that can lead an individual to reassess his or her lifestyle and move toward something healthier. For all of us in Western democracies, this crisis is "a chance to take a look at ourselves, our banking systems, and our politicians and make some changes." This will mean doing what we can to pressure our governments to make changes in the way financial institutions do business so that a bust like this is less likely to happen. But, he insists:

> the level of our individual response is just as important. On that level, we have to start thinking about when we have sufficient—sufficient money, sufficient stuff—and whether we really need the things we think we do, beyond what we already have. In a world running out of resources, the most important ethical, political, and ecological idea can be summed up in one simple word: "enough."[53]

As friends of God, we can and need to discuss honestly with God and one another issues of lifestyle. Reading a book like Lanchester's gave me some talking points for my prayer and led to a greater willingness to question how I use things and how I contribute to the detriment of the environment. Such conversations need not lead to anxious concern about lifestyle; in fact, if anxious concern is the result, you might want to examine how that happened. Most often, anxious concern does not lead to any real changes, only to a spiral of self-absorbing questions to which we rarely find answers. Real dialogue with God usually leads to changes in behavior that are freeing and life enhancing. Such dialogue will give us the insight and the courage to say the simple word *enough*. In the process, we shall become part of the solution rather than part of the problem.

12

Always, Gratitude

*Giving thanks to God the Father at all
time and for everything.*

—EPHESIANS 5:20

Have you ever wondered how God reacts when we accept
the offer of friendship and cooperate in the divine work of
making the world new? Just recently, a Jesuit I know heard
Jesus say, "I'm grateful that you want to be my companion,
and my Father is grateful too." I have sensed God's gratitude as well. I know that this sounds strange; after all Jesus
once said:

> Who among you would say to your slave who has just
> come in from plowing or tending sheep in the field,
> "Come here at once and take your place at the table?"
> Would you not rather say to him, "Prepare supper for
> me, put on your apron and serve me while I eat and
> drink; later you may eat and drink?" Do you thank the
> slave for doing what was commanded? So you also, when

you have done all that you were ordered to do, say, "We are worthless slaves; we have done only what we ought to have done!" (Luke 17:7–10)

It seems to me that Jesus intends this parable as an antidote to believing that we deserve gratitude from God. It cannot mean that God treats us as slaves; in fact, he calls us to friendship. If you had a friend who helped you out in some project, wouldn't you be grateful? Well, why can't we accept gratitude from God? Not everyone accepts the offer of friendship; wouldn't it be strange if God were not grateful to those who do?

However, I want only to allude to God's gratitude here; the more important thing for us is to know how *we* are reacting as we engage in this divine relationship. What is your predominant feeling toward God right now? If you tried to do the Contemplation for Attaining Love described in chapter 2, you must have been filled with gratitude for all that you have received from God. This gratitude leads to love for God, which is the aim of the exercise.

To believe in God means to believe that the whole universe and everything in it exists only because of God's bounteous love and desire. Even a glimpse of this truth has to leave us singing with gratitude. The refrain of the hymn "How Can I Keep from Singing," expresses how we feel when we catch that glimpse of God's lavish love for us:

No storm can shake my inmost calm,
While to this rock I'm clinging.
Since Love is Lord of heaven and earth,
How can I keep from singing?

I began this book two years ago. Work on it was interrupted by other obligations and was slowed when I ran into roadblocks in the writing. At times it has been hard work; indeed, at one point, I thought that I couldn't bring it to completion because it just wasn't coming together. But each time I began to write, I prayed the prayer of St. Anselm that I often use with writing projects and that I put on the first page of the computer text (now in the front of the book) to remind me of what was most important. Now as I come to the book's end, I find myself filled with gratitude that I have been able to complete the book at least to my satisfaction. I do not feel that I deserve God's gratitude, but I will happily receive it if it is offered.

I keep praying, "I believe, help my unbelief." By "belief" here I mean belief in God on whom everything that exists depends. When I am given the gift of belief, I am filled with gratitude and wonder that I exist at all; that I am still alive; that I am capable of doing anything, let alone writing a book. Belief in God leads to gratitude as the only appropriate response. In *Franny and Zooey*, J. D. Salinger describes a conversation between Zooey and his mother while Zooey is shaving. His mother wonders whether Franny, Zooey's sister, needs to see a psychoanalyst. Zooey gets serious and says:

> For a psychoanalyst to be any good with Franny at all, he'd have to be a pretty peculiar type. I don't know. He'd have to believe that it was through the grace of God that he'd been inspired to study psychoanalysis in the first place. He'd have to believe that it was through the grace of God that he wasn't run over by a goddam truck before he ever even got his license to practice. He'd have to believe that it's through the grace of God that he has the native intelligence to be able to help his goddam patients at all. I don't know any *good* analysts who think along those lines. But that's the only kind of psychoanalyst who might be able to do Franny any good at all.[54]

The kind of psychoanalyst Zooey describes fits the way I feel as I come to the end of this work. I am filled with gratitude that I have been able to finish it and, in anticipation, that you want to read it. And so I can say with St. Paul:

> I thank my God every time I remember you, constantly praying with joy in every one of my prayers for all of you, because of your sharing in the gospel from the first day until now. I am confident of this, that the one who began

a good work among you will bring it to completion by the day of Jesus Christ.

It is right for me to think this way about all of you, because you hold me in your heart, for all of you share in God's grace with me, both in my imprisonment and in the defense and confirmation of the gospel. For God is my witness, how I long for all of you with the compassion of Christ Jesus.

And this is my prayer, that your love may overflow more and more with knowledge and full insight to help you to determine what is best, so that in the day of Christ you may be pure and blameless, having produced the harvest of righteousness that comes through Jesus Christ for the glory and praise of God. (Philippians 1:3–11)

Coda

In Luke's Gospel, Jesus enters Jerusalem for the last time, riding on a donkey and weeping. I invite you to listen to this scene from Jesus' perspective. He believes that he is the Messiah, the only one ever to be, who ushers in the final chapter of the fulfillment of God's dream. He is the way, the truth, and the life; there is no other way to be human than his way. He has desperately tried to convince his people of this reality, but they have not wanted to repent and believe the good news. Now listen to what Luke writes:

> As he came near and saw the city, he wept over it, saying, "If you, even you, had only recognized on this day the things that make for peace! But now they are hidden from your eyes. Indeed, the days will come upon you, when your enemies will set up ramparts around you and surround you, and hem you in on every side. They will crush you to the ground, you and your children within you, and they will not leave within you one stone upon another; because you did not recognize the time of your visitation from God." (Luke 19:41–44)

Jesus is heartbroken that God's own people have not accepted God's risk, that they have not known what was for their peace and for the peace of the world. He weeps because they still do not get that God wants their friendship, not their rivalry or their subservience or their willingness to fight battles for God.

Now imagine Jesus looking down on Washington, D.C., or any other city of our world. Imagine Jesus looking down on your city or town. Is he still weeping that we have not known the things that make for peace? I sense that he is. What will wipe those tears away? You and I, and all of us together, can accept the offer of friendship and help wipe the tears away. To be a friend of God is not easy; a spirituality of friendship does not bring cheap grace. God has taken the risk of creating us for friendship and even of joining us in this world of tears and joys. Could there be anything better to do with your life than to accept God's offer of friendship, to participate in the dream of a planet where the lion and the lamb, the Jew and the Palestinian, the Muslim, the Buddhist, the animist, the atheist, and the Christian sit down together? I cannot think of anything better. Can you?

Suggestions for Spiritual Growth

Rabbi Abraham Heschel is reported to have told a story about a rabbi who asked his students how they could tell when night had ended and day had come. One student asked, "Could it be when you could see an animal in the distance and tell whether it is a sheep or a dog?" "No," said the rabbi. "Could it be when you can look at a tree in the distance and tell whether it is a fig tree or a peach tree?" Again the rabbi said no. The students demanded to know the answer. "It is when you look at the face of any man and woman and see that she or he is your sister and brother, because, if you cannot do this, then no matter what time it is, it is still night."[55]

Heschel clearly takes seriously the story of Genesis. God is the creator and father of everyone who exists, hence, we are all brothers and sisters. And until I come to recognize this fact and make it a way of life, then, in effect, it is night. I am not living in communion with God, and I am blinded from seeing the world as it truly is. Of course, in this blindness I am joined by most of my sisters and brothers, and almost every culture we grow up in seems to teach us to live in the night.

No doubt about it, living as daughters and sons of God—and expressing truly the divine image—is not easy in a world in which God's values so often run counter to the cultural values that shape us. How can we become more forgiving, more compassionate, more unafraid as we go about the daily business of our lives?

Essentially, we are asking, How do I grow up spiritually? How do I mature as a human being, to become what I was created to become? To answer this question would take another book or two. But let me point you in some useful directions in this short appendix.

Jesus says, "Love one another as I have loved you." We can develop spiritually (and, really, in every way) by getting to know Jesus as an intimate friend. He has called us friends and wants us to reciprocate. In *A Friendship Like No Other* and *What Do I Want in Prayer?* I have provided exercises that you can use to grow in friendship with God and with Jesus, God's son.[56]

What these books suggest is that growing into friendship with God requires the same discipline as growing into a deep friendship with anyone. You have to spend time with Jesus in order to know and love him and thus grow more like him in your mind, heart, and action. But spending such time only responds to the deepest desire of our hearts. In desiring us into being, God has only our best interests at heart; and our best interests, both as individuals and as a people, lie in all of us developing our relationship with God. If you have gotten this far, you already know that your heart's deepest desire is for friendship with God. Trust that desire, and start spending time with God each day.

The amount of time does not have to be long; all that is required is to spend whatever time you can find regularly. And pay attention to what happens as you spend time with God. As I mentioned in chapter 3, paying attention to what goes on in our minds and hearts is the best way to learn the ways of God. The references to discernment of spirits in that chapter will help you make more sense of these movements of heart and mind. Gradually, God will draw you into a deeper friendship in which you will learn by osmosis how to allow God's image to come alive in you day by day.

Some Web sites can be of help. For example, Creighton University in Omaha, Nebraska, has a Web site that offers suggestions for daily prayer and other resources, including a retreat in daily life that takes you through the Spiritual Exercises of St. Ignatius of Loyola. Millions have found Sacred Space helpful, a Web site maintained by the Jesuits of Ireland. Once you have started on this kind of search, you will find many other helps.[57]

It also helps to be able to talk with others about this journey into a deeper friendship with God. You might keep an eye open for others who are on the same journey with whom you can meet on a fairly regular basis to talk about your experiences and thus help and encourage one another. Ask around in your parish or among friends or see what is available on the Internet.

A spiritual director is also helpful. Increasingly people from all walks of life have been trained as spiritual directors. Admittedly, you should remember the caveat "buyer beware"—not everyone who offers him- or herself as a spiritual director is competent—but that caveat should not keep you from asking around among people you trust for the names of competent spiritual directors. The ones I find most helpful are those who are deeply interested in God and God's mysterious ways and who thus want to hear about your experiences of encountering God. You don't want a spiritual director who tells you what you should experience but one who wants to hear your experience and to help you make sense of it so that you engage in your relationship with God with increasing passion and understanding.

As you can see from these suggestions, we do not grow spiritually in isolation from other people. We are made for relationships with God and with one another. In fact, persons are defined by relationships; in this, we mirror God, who is a trinity of "persons" united in bonds of friendship. So we are made for community. A community of faith that becomes a real community of shared faith and experience is the ideal for every church entity. I encourage you not only to look for such communities of faith but also to become active in fostering such communities in the churches to which you belong.

Appendix 2

Rummaging for God: Praying Backward through Your Day

BY DENNIS HAMM, SJ

About 20 years ago, at breakfast and during the few hours that followed, I had a small revelation. This happened while I was living in a small community of five Jesuits, all graduate students in New Haven, Connecticut. I was alone in the kitchen, with my cereal and the *New York Times*, when another Jesuit came in and said: "I had the weirdest dream just before I woke up. It was a liturgical dream. The lector had just read the first reading and proceeded to announce, 'The responsorial refrain today is, *If at first you don't succeed, try, try again.*' Whereupon the entire congregation soberly repeated, '*If at first you don't succeed, try, try again.*'" We both thought this enormously funny. At first, I wasn't sure just why this was so humorous. After all, almost everyone would assent to the courageous truth of the maxim, "If at first . . ." It has to be a cross-cultural truism ("Keep on truckin'!"). Why, then, would these words sound so incongruous in a liturgy?

A little later in the day, I stumbled onto a clue. Another, similar phrase popped into my mind: "If today you hear his voice, harden not your hearts" (Psalm 95). It struck me that that sentence has exactly the same rhythm and the same syntax as: "If at first you don't succeed, try, try again." Both begin with an *if*, clause and end in an imperative. Both have seven beats. Maybe that was one of the unconscious sources of the humor.

The try-try-again statement *sounds*, like the harden-not-your-hearts refrain, yet what a contrast! The latter is clearly biblical, a paraphrase of a verse from a psalm, one frequently used as a responsorial refrain at the Eucharist. The former, you know instinctively, is probably not in the Bible, not even in Proverbs. It is true enough, as far as it goes, but it does not go far enough. There is nothing of faith in it, no sense of God. The sentiment of the line from Psalm 95, however, expresses a conviction central to Hebrew and Christian faith, that we live a life in dialogue with God. The contrast between those two seven-beat lines has, ever since, been for me a paradigm illustrating that truth.

Yet how do we hear the voice of God? Our Christian tradition has at least four answers to that question. First, along with the faithful of most religions, we perceive the divine in what God has made, creation itself (that insight sits at the heart of Christian moral thinking). Second, we hear

God's voice in the Scriptures, which we even *call*, "the word of God." Third, we hear God in the authoritative teaching of the church, the living tradition of our believing community. Finally, we hear God by attending to our experience, and interpreting it in the light of all those other ways of hearing the divine voice—the structures of creation, the Bible, the living tradition of the community.

The phrase, "If *today*, you hear his voice," implies that the divine voice must somehow be accessible in our daily experience, for we are creatures who live one day at a time. If God wants to communicate with us, it has to happen in the course of a 24-hour day, for we live in no other time. And how do we go about this kind of listening? Long tradition has provided a helpful tool, which we call the "examination of consciousness" today. "Rummaging for God" is an expression that suggests going through a drawer full of stuff, feeling around, looking for something that you are sure must be in there somewhere. I think that image catches some of the feel of what is classically known in church language as the prayer of "examen."

The *examen*, or examination, of conscience is an ancient practice in the church. In fact, even before Christianity, the Pythagoreans and the Stoics promoted a version of the practice. It is what most of us Catholics were taught to do to prepare for confession. In that form, the examen, was a matter of examining one's life in terms of the Ten Commandments to see how daily behavior stacked up against those divine criteria. St. Ignatius includes it as one of the exercises in his manual *The Spiritual Exercises.*

It is still a salutary thing to do but wears thin as a life-long, daily practice. It is hard to motivate yourself to keep searching your experience for how you sinned. In recent decades, spiritual writers have worked with the implication that conscience in Romance languages like French (*conscience*) and Spanish (*conciencia*) means more than our English word *conscience*, in the sense of moral awareness and judgment; it also means "consciousness."

Now prayer that deals with the full contents of your *consciousness*, lets you cast your net much more broadly than prayer that limits itself to the contents of conscience, or moral awareness. A number of people—most famously, George Aschenbrenner, SJ, in an article in *Review for Religious*, (1971)—have developed this idea in profoundly practical ways. Recently, the Institute of Jesuit Sources in St. Louis published a fascinating reflection by Joseph Tetlow, SJ, called *The Most Postmodern Prayer: American Jesuit Identity and the Examen of Conscience, 1920-1990.*

What I am proposing here is a way of doing the examen that works for me. It puts a special emphasis on feelings, for reasons that I hope will become apparent. First, I describe the format. Second, I invite you to spend a few minutes actually doing it. Third, I describe some of the consequences that I have discovered to flow from this kind of prayer.

Consequences.

1. Pray for light. Since we are not simply daydreaming or reminiscing but rather looking for some sense of how the Spirit of God is leading us, it only makes sense to pray for some illumination. The goal is not simply memory but graced understanding. That's a gift from God devoutly to be begged. "Lord, help me understand this blooming, buzzing confusion."

2. Review the day in thanksgiving. Note how different this is from looking immediately for your sins. Nobody likes to poke around in the memory bank to uncover smallness, weakness, lack of generosity. But everybody likes to fondle beautiful gifts, and that is precisely what the past 24 hours contain—gifts of existence, work-relationships, food, challenges. Gratitude is the foundation of our whole relationship with God. So use whatever cues help you to walk through the day from the moment of awakening—even the dreams you recall upon awakening. Walk through the past 24 hours, from hour to hour, from place to place, task to task, person to person, thanking the Lord for every gift you encounter.

3. Review the feelings that surface in the replay of the day. Our feelings, positive and negative, the painful and the pleasing, are clear signals of where the action was during the day. Simply pay attention to any and all of those feelings as they surface, the whole range: delight, boredom, fear, anticipation, resentment, anger, peace, contentment, impatience, desire, hope, regret, shame, uncertainty, compassion, disgust, gratitude, pride, rage, doubt, confidence, admiration, shyness—whatever was there. Some of us may be hesitant to focus on feelings in this over-psychologized age, but I believe that these feelings are the liveliest index to what is happening in our lives. This leads us to the fourth moment:

4. Choose one of those feelings (positive or negative) and pray from it. That is, choose the remembered feeling that most caught your attention. The feeling is a sign that something important was going on. Now simply express spontaneously the prayer that surfaces as you attend to the source of the feeling: praise, petition, contrition, cry for help or healing, whatever.

5. Look toward tomorrow. Using your appointment calendar if that helps, face your immediate future. What feelings surface as you look at the tasks, meetings, and appointments that face you? Fear? Delighted anticipation? Self-doubt? Temptation to procrastination? Zestful planning? Regret? Weakness? Whatever it is, turn it into prayer—for help, for healing, whatever comes spontaneously. To round off the examen, say the Lord's Prayer. A mnemonic for recalling the five points: LT3F (light, thanks, feelings, focus, future).

Do it.

Take a few minutes each day to pray through the past 24 hours, and toward the next 24 hours, with that five-point format.

Consequences.

Here are some of the consequences flowing from this kind of prayer.

1. There is always something to pray about. For a person who does this kind of prayer at least once a day, there is never the question: What should I talk to God about? Until you die, you always have a past 24 hours, and you always have some feelings about what's next.

2. The gratitude moment is worthwhile in itself. "Dedicate yourselves to gratitude," Paul tells the Colossians. Even if we drift off into slumber after reviewing the gifts of the day, we have praised the Lord.

3. We learn to face the Lord where we are, as we are. There is no other way to be present to God, of course, but we often fool ourselves into thinking that we have to put on our best face before we address our God.

4. We learn to respect our feelings. Feelings count. They are morally neutral until we make some choice about acting upon or dealing with them. But if we don't attend to them, we miss what they have to tell us about the quality of our lives.

5. Praying from feelings, we are liberated from them. An unattended emotion can dominate and manipulate us. Attending to and praying from and about the persons and situations that give rise to the emotions help us to cease being unwitting slaves of our emotions.

6. We actually find something to bring to confession. That is, we stumble across our sins without making them the primary focus.

7. We can experience an inner healing. People have found that praying about (as opposed to fretting about or denying) feelings leads to a healing of mental life. We probably get a head start on our dreamwork when we do this.

8. This kind of prayer helps us get over our Deism. Deism is belief in a sort of clock-maker God, a God who does indeed exist but does not have much, if anything, to do with his people's ongoing life. The God we have come to know through our Jewish and Christian experience is more present than we actually think.

9. Praying this way is an antidote to the spiritual disease of Pelagianism. Pelagianism was the heresy that approached life with God as a do-it-yourself project ("If at first you don't succeed . . ."), whereas a true theology of grace and freedom sees life as response to God's love ("If today you hear God's voice . . .").

A final thought. How can anyone dare to say that paying attention to felt experience is a listening to the voice of God? On the face of it, it does sound like a dangerous presumption. But, notice, I am not equating memory with the voice of God. I am saying that, if we are to listen for the God who creates and sustains us, we need to take seriously and prayerfully the meeting between the creatures we are and all else that God holds lovingly in existence. That interface is the felt experience of my day. It deserves prayerful attention. It is a big part of how we know and respond to God.

This article first appeared in *America*, May 14, 1994

Notes

1. St. Ignatius of Loyola, "Spiritual Exercises," in *Personal Writings*, trans. and ed. Joseph A. Munitiz and Philip Endean (London: Penguin Books, 1996), 329–330. (All citations to the *Spiritual Exercises*, abbreviated S.E., herein are taken from this work).

2. Gerard Manley Hopkins, "God's Grandeur," in *Gerard Manley Hopkins: The Oxford Authors*, edited by Catherine Phillips (Oxford: Oxford University Press, 1986), 128.

3. Frances M. Young, *Brokenness and Blessing: Towards a Biblical Spirituality* (Grand Rapids, MI: Baker Academic, 2007), 32.

4. C. S. Lewis, *The Screwtape Letters* (New York: Macmillan, 1962), 3.

5. John Macmurray, *Freedom in the Modern World* (London: Faber and Faber, 1968), 24.

6. William A. Barry, *A Friendship Like No Other: Experiencing God's Amazing Embrace* (Chicago: Loyola Press, 2008); see also William A. Barry, *Here's My Heart, Here's My Hand: Living Fully in Friendship with God* (Chicago: Loyola Press, 2009).

7. Kyriacos C. Markides, *The Mountain of Silence: A Search for Orthodox Spirituality* (New York: Doubleday Image, 2001), 143–45.

8. References for discernment of spirits: William A. Barry, SJ, "How Do I Know I'm Experiencing God?", in *A Friendship Like No Other: Experiencing God's Amazing Embrace* (Chicago: Loyola Press, 2008), 177–191; Maureen Conroy, *The Discerning Heart: Discovering a Personal God* (Chicago: Loyola University

Press, 1993); J. Michael Sparough, SJ, Tim Hipskind, SJ, and Jim Manney, *What's Your Decision? How to Make Choices with Clarity and Confidence* (Chicago: Loyola Press, 2010); Timothy M. Gallagher, *The Discernment of Spirits: An Ignatian Guide for Everyday Living* (New York: Crossroad 2005); Timothy M. Gallagher, *Spiritual Consolation: An Ignatian Guide for the Greater Discernment of Spirits* (New York: Crossroad, 2007).

9. Rodney Stark, *The Rise of Christianity: How the Obscure, Marginal Jesus Movement Became the Dominant Religious Force in the Western World in a Few Centuries* (San Francisco: HarperSanFrancisco, 1996).

10. Barbara J. Kouba, "'I Love You for Hating Me,'" *America*, August 17–24, 2009, 26–28.

11. Garson Kanin, *Atlantic*, March 1964.

12. Elias Chacour, *We Belong to the Land* (New York: HarperCollins, 1990), 30–32.

13. Jean Sulivan, *Eternity, My Beloved*, trans. Sr. Francis Ellen Riordan (St. Paul, MN: River Boat Books, 1998), 125–26.

14. Dennis Hamm, "Rummaging for God: Praying Backward through Your Day," *America*, May 14, 1994, 22–23.

15. John Macmurray, *To Save from Fear* (Philadelphia: Wider Quaker Fellowship, 1990), 4.

16. Alcoholics Anonymous, *Alcoholics Anonymous: The Story of How Many Thousands of Men and Women Have Recovered from Alcoholism*, 3rd ed. (New York: Alcoholics Anonymous World Services, 1976).

17. Kyriacos C. Markides, *The Mountain of Silence: A Search for Orthodox Spirituality* (New York: Doubleday Image, 2001), 77.

18. Gerard E. Goggins, *Anonymous Disciple* (Worcester, MA: Assumption Communications, 1995), 167–68.

19. Franz Wright, "One Heart," in *Walking to Martha's Vineyard* (New York: Alfred A. Knopf, 2004), 5 (reprinted with permission of author).

20. Samuel P. Huntington, *The Class of Civilizations: Remaking of the World Order* (New York: Simon and Schuster, 1996).

21. L. Gregory Jones, *Embodying Forgiveness: A Theological Analysis* (Grand Rapids, MI: William B. Eerdmans, 1995), 120.

22. Ibid., 122.

23. Miroslav Volf, *Exclusion and Embrace: A Theological Exploration of Identity, Otherness, and Reconciliation* (Nashville, TN: Abingdon Press, 1996), 9.

24. Desmond Mpilo Tutu, *No Future without Forgiveness* (New York: Doubleday Image, 1999).

25. Miroslav Volf, *Free of Charge: Giving and Forgiving in a Culture Stripped of Grace* (Grand Rapids, MI: Zondervan, 2005), 161.

26. Stephen Yavorsky, "You Look at Them; I'll Look at You," *Human Development* 29, no. 2 (2008): 9–10.

27. Robert Weber, "Searching for the Curative Power of Gratitude and Forgiveness in Groups," *Group Circle: The Newsletter of the American Group Psychotherapy Association*, Fall 2005, 1.

28. Miroslav Volf, *Free of Charge*; Miroslav Volf, *The End of Memory: Remembering Rightly in a Violent World* (Grand Rapids, MI: William B. Eerdmans, 2006); L. Gregory Jones, *Embodying Forgiveness*; N. T. Wright, *Evil and the Justice of God* (Downers Grove, IL: InterVarsity Press, 2006).

29. L. Gregory Jones, *Embodying Forgiveness*, 218.

30. Desmond Mpilo Tutu, *No Future without Forgiveness* (New York: Doubleday Image, 1999), 150–151.

31. Alex Perry, "Letting Bygones Be Bygones," *Time*, March 1, 2007.

32. Matt Garr, "A Difficult Future for National Reconciliation," *Human Development* 29, no. 3 (2008): 26–31; John Katunga Murhula, "Prospects of Reconciliation: The Case of the Democratic Republic of Congo," *Human Development* 29, no. 3 (2008), 33–44.

33. Raymond G. Helmick, SJ, "The 'Hard Men' as Peacemakers," *Human Development* 29, no. 3 (2008), 22.

34. William A. Barry, "Toward Communal Discernment," in *Letting God Come Close: An Approach to the Ignatian Spiritual Exercises* (Chicago: Loyola Press, 2001).

35. Susan Kay, "Would You Do the Same Today?" *Human Development* 29, no. 2 (2008): 48 (with permission of the author).

36. Edward Niziolek, "Compassion and Peace," *O Miraculous Wonder Help Us to Find You: Book II* (Arlington Heights, MA: Stephen Surette Graphic Services, 2008), 61.

37. Tracy Kidder, in *Strength in What Remains: A Journey of Remembrance and Forgiveness* (New York: Random House, 2009), 126–30.

38. Richard H. Bell, *Simone Weil: The Way of Justice as Compassion* (Lanham, MD: Rowman and Littlefield, 1988), 85.

39. John Macmurray, *Persons in Relation* (Atlantic Highlands, NJ: Humanities Press, 1979), 159.

40. Richard H. Bell, *Simone Weil: The Way of Justice as Compassion* (Lanham, MD: Rowman and Littlefield, 1988), 49–50.

41. Tracy Kidder, in *Strength in What Remains: A Journey of Remembrance and Forgiveness* (New York: Random House, 2009), 10–14.

42. N. T. Wright, *Surprised by Hope: Rethinking Heaven, the Resurrection, and the Mission of the Church* (New York: HarperOne, 2008), 208.

43. Charles Taylor, *A Secular Age* (Cambridge, MA: Harvard University Press, 2007), 3, 74–75.

44. Kyriacos C. Markides, *The Mountain of Silence: A Search for Orthodox Spirituality* (New York: Doubleday Image, 2001), 148.

45. Rebecca Solnit, *A Paradise Built in Hell: The Extraordinary Communities That Arise in Disaster* (New York: Viking, 2009), 188.

46. Robert Louis Wilken, *The Spirit of Early Christian Thought* (New Haven, CT: Yale University Press, 2003), 192.

47. Kyriacos C. Markides, *The Mountain of Silence: A Search for Orthodox Spirituality* (New York: Doubleday Image, 2001), 148.

48. Pope Benedict XVI, *Encyclical Letter Caritas in Veritate*, Holy See, http://www.vatican.va/holy_father/benedict_xvi/encyc licals/documents/hf_ben-xvi_enc_20090629_caritas-in -veritate_en.html.

49. Robert Louis Wilken, *The Spirit of Early Christian Thought* (New Haven, CT: Yale University Press, 2003), 210.

50. John Lanchester, *I.O.U.: Why Everyone Owes Everyone and No One Can Pay* (New York: Simon and Schuster, 2010), 217.

51. Ibid., 214–215.

52. Ibid.

53. Ibid., 232.

54. J. D. Salinger, *Franny and Zooey* (Toronto: Bantam Books), 109.

55. Cited in Alfred McBride, O.Carm., "A Sturdy Framework," *America*, September 28, 2009, 16.

56. William A. Barry, *A Friendship Like No Other: Experiencing God's Amazing Embrace* (Chicago: Loyola Press, 2008); William A. Barry, *What Do I Want in Prayer?* (New York: Paulist, 1994).

57. Creighton University Web site: Type Creighton University Ministry on your search engine and there you will find a side bar referring to online services. Sacred Space Web site: Type Sacred Space on your search engine.

Annotated Bibliography

Alexander, Andy, Maureen McCann Waldron, and Larry Gillick. *Retreat in the Real World: Finding Intimacy with God Wherever You Are*. Chicago: Loyola Press, 2009. With photographs by Don Doll, SJ, this fine book offers readers a chance to grow in intimacy with God by adapting the Spiritual Exercises of St. Ignatius of Loyola for busy people who can devote some time each day to prayer.

Barry, William A. *A Friendship Like No Other: Experiencing God's Amazing Embrace*. Chicago: Loyola Press, 2008.

Barry, William A. *Here's My Heart, Here's My Hand: Living Fully in Friendship with God*. Chicago: Loyola Press, 2009.

Ellsberg, Robert. *The Saints' Guide to Happiness: Everyday Wisdom from the Lives of the Saints*. New York: North Point Press, 2003. An engaging and insightful read.

Jones, L. Gregory. *Embodying Forgiveness: A Theological Analysis*. Grand Rapids, MI: William B. Eerdmans, 1995. A profound theological work that also is practical.

Markides, Kyriacos C. *The Mountain of Silence: A Search for Orthodox Spirituality*. New York: Doubleday Image, 2001. A surprisingly good introduction to Greek Orthodox spirituality by a sociologist at the University of Maine.

Martin, James. *My Life with the Saints*. Chicago: Loyola Press, 2006. A wonderfully engaging introduction to the saints by one of today's best spiritual writers.

Solnit, Rebecca. *A Paradise Built in Hell: The Extraordinary Communities That Arise in Disaster.* New York: Viking, 2009. Stories of how ordinary people react in disasters—they will give you hope for our race.

Taylor, Barbara Brown. *An Altar in the World: A Geography of Faith.* New York: HarperOne, 2009. Offers a variety of spiritual practices in an engaging and grounded way.

Taylor, Barbara Brown. *Leaving Church: A Memoir of Faith.* New York: HarperOne, 2006. A well-written, down-to-earth story of the author's tenure as pastor of a small-town Episcopal parish.

Volf, Miroslav. *The End of Memory: Remembering Rightly in a Violent World.* Grand Rapids, MI: William B. Eerdmans, 2006. The author uses his own experience of being abused as a prisoner to develop a theological account of how forgiveness involves forgetting.

Volf, Miroslav. *Exclusion and Embrace: A Theological Exploration of Identity, Otherness, and Reconciliation.* Nashville, TN: Abingdon Press, 1996. A dense but well-written theological exploration of the need and the difficulty of forgiveness.

Wright, N. T. *Surprised by Hope: Rethinking Heaven, the Resurrection, and the Mission of the Church.* New York: HarperOne, 2008. I read anything Bishop Wright writes whether as N. T. or Tom. An engaging, deeply committed, and very knowledgeable writer.

Wright, Vinita Hampton. *Days of Deepening Friendship: For the Woman Who Wants Authentic Life with God.* Chicago: Loyola Press, 2009. A user-friendly guide for women seekers.

Young, Frances M. *Brokenness and Blessing: Towards a Biblical Spirituality.* Grand Rapids, MI: Baker Academic, 2007. A lovely and enlightening book on how suffering can become a blessing.

Other books
by William A. Barry, SJ

God's Passionate Desire

$14.95 • 2703-5 • Paperback

In *God's Passionate Desire*, Fr. Barry helps us understand the foundations of our relationship with God. In his warm, conversational style, Barry offers meditations, poses questions, and gently encourages us to respond to God's immeasurable love by following what is truly in each of our hearts—a longing for an intimate relationship with God.

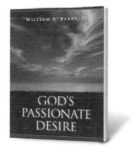

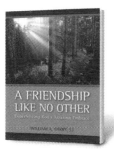

A Friendship Like No Other

$14.95 • 2702-8 • Paperback

A Friendship Like No Other explores the idea that God wants to relate to us as a close friend. Grounded in biblical tradition and with a clear focus on Ignatian spirituality, this book offers a fresh, heart-changing approach to living joyfully in the freedom of God's embrace.

Here's My Heart, Here's My Hand
$14.95 • 2807-0 • Paperback

After accepting the premise that God wants our friendship, *Here's My Heart, Here's My Hand* helps the reader engage in this relationship. This book is ideal both for spiritual seekers and for those who already know the joy of a relationship with God but want to strengthen that friendship.

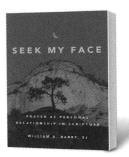

Seek My Face
$13.95 • 2808-7 • Paperback

Seek My Face focuses on various Old and New Testament events and personalities—Abraham, Moses, Peter, and more—to help readers understand the many ways in which we can enter into an intimate relationship with God as well as with Jesus and the Holy Spirit.